EN-LIGHTEN UP

ENHANCE YOUR MIND.
ENHANCE YOUR HUMAN CONNECTIONS.
ENHANCE YOUR LIFE.

Jingzhi Meng,

Best,

Bob Kittell

INDIGORIVER
PUBLISHING

EN-LIGHTEN UP

ENHANCE YOUR MIND.
ENHANCE YOUR HUMAN CONNECTIONS.
ENHANCE YOUR LIFE.

BOB KITTELL

STRESS LESS TO SUCCESS

Indigo River Publishing

En-Lighten Up
Copyright © 2020 by Bob Kittell

Editors: Thomas Cantrell, Jackson Haynes, and Regina Cornell
Book Design: Robin Vuchnich

Indigo River Publishing
3 West Garden Street, Suite 718
Pensacola, FL 32502
www.indigoriverpublishing.com

Ordering Information:
Quantity sales: Special discounts are available on quantity purchases by corporations, associations, and others. For details, contact the publisher at the address above.

Orders by US trade bookstores and wholesalers: Please contact the publisher at the address above.

Printed in the United States of America

Library of Congress Control Number: 2020944648
ISBN: 978-1-950906-78-9

First Edition

*With Indigo River Publishing, you can always expect great books, strong voices, and meaningful messages. Most importantly, you'll always find...*words worth reading.

Dedicated to my children and yours – and to business and civic leaders, professors, teachers and students everywhere.

If the rest of the world catches on . . . *great!*

TABLE OF CONTENTS

FOREWORD

All of my dreams came true.

They did.

My life turned out bigger—much bigger—and better than I ever could have imagined.

Then it fell to pieces, nearly ending tragically as I sat in my room wondering if I should turn out the lights forever—for no good reason except to end the pain.

My pursuit of success was intense. I had it all...and lost most of it. I experienced massive panic attacks, deep anxiety, dark depression—all while continuing to present to thousands of people and living behind the mask of "everything is just great!"

Is this book about reaching the top, tumbling into the abyss, then crawling out again? Is it about rising to a new awareness of life and a deeper connection with others? Is this about cancer, divorce, death, determination, resilience, survival, and success? Yes, it's about all of these. And, no, it's not. In fact, it's not about me at all.

This book is really about you.

Have you experienced bright, exciting ups and then dark, depressing downs? Do you know someone who has been there or may be there right now? Perhaps my story will make a difference for you or someone you know. I hope so. I don't have all the answers, but I may have some.

Walk with me on my life's journey; share my struggle to the top as an accomplished stage presenter and an expert in memory and mind mastery, and then my fall into the cluttered, chaotic depths of a dark, depressive Hell, then the rise once again, this time into a clear, calm awareness of Heaven—right here, right now.

My journey brought me a new sense of hope and a calming mindfulness that I would like to share with you, and perhaps you will share it with others.

CHAPTER ONE

The Monumental Moment of Motivation

"We need to set our course by the stars, not by the light of every passing ship."

—Omar Bradley

I am speaking alongside former Prime Minister Margaret Thatcher, former First Lady Barbara Bush, and the famous Zig Ziglar at the San Diego Arena as part of the Get Motivated! tour, with 12,000 in attendance. *How did this happen? How did I get here? How is it that I am sharing the stage with these amazing people?* Prime Minister Thatcher has just finished speaking, and I'm up next.

How did *this happen?*

In the coming years, I was the leadoff speaker at events all over the country—events featuring Donald Trump, Anthony Robbins, and Robert Kiyosaki.

How did this *happen?*

Well, it goes back to 1975 when I was seventeen years old and had one pair of school pants that better last me the whole year. One day my dad invited me to go to work with him. The first thing I learned was that they don't air condition steel plants in the summer time. It was miserable in there. For years, I had been giving my father a hard time—like a lot of teenagers do. But the day I walked into that plant with him was the last day I ever gave him a hard time—about anything. I had no idea what he endured to support his family. He had, and still has, my deepest respect.

The plant was hot, stifling, miserably oppressive, and deafeningly loud, so loud my ears were ringing at the end of the day. My father was nearly deaf after years of working there. But he was proud of his work at P&G Steel in Buffalo, New York, and he wanted to share that sense of American industry with me.

"Son, if you can't get into college," he said cheerfully, "I might be able to pull some strings and get you a job working with me, right here, in the factory."

I was appalled. *Oh no! No way!*

That was my first real exposure to a motivational message. I was motivated to figure out a way to never get stuck working in that place. In fact, I was highly motivated to never work anywhere I didn't want to work. I was more than motivated, I was terrified; terrified at the idea of ever being sucked into doing something I hated—for the rest of my life.

This was a pivotal moment.

And this is my story of preparation, opportunity, and action—the three aspects that opened doors and brought me to stages that were so much bigger than the son of a steel worker could ever dream of.

***

In today's society, a lot of people wonder why memorization is important, when they can just look up the information they need on the internet. Can you go to the internet to remember the twenty items you need from the grocery store? Can you go to the internet to remember the name of the potential business associate you just met at the coffee shop? How about to remember a long number, like your bank account number? The internet cannot help you remember these aspects of your life that you use daily. Throughout this book, you will learn several different kinds of memory techniques, and if you use them, you will not only strengthen your mind, you will improve your daily life.

Your brain is a mental filing system. You just need to learn the correct way to file information and how to easily recall it when you need to.

I have memorized over a hundred and fifty inspirational quotations by filing them away in my brain, and I can recall them in order anytime I need to. I actually perform this exercise onstage in front of a live audience to prove how advanced my memory training is. I'll number the quotations 1–50 on a giant projector behind me, ask the audience to call out a number, and then iterate the inspirational quotation. Then I'll project quotes 51–100 and ask the audience to call out another number. Again, I reach into my brain, pull out the file of the number they have called, and recite the quotation. Once more, with quotes 101–150, I correctly announce the quotation someone calls out and thus convince the audience that my memory techniques work!

Memorizing inspirational quotations and filing them away in your brain does more than just strengthen your mind; it floods your consciousness with inspirational messages that flash up throughout your life whenever you may need them. For instance, whenever I picked up my children, quote 130 flashed in my mind:

> *"Children are like wet cement. Whatever falls on them makes an impression."* —Haim Ginott

Or quote 133:

> *"Children are not things to be molded but people to be unfolded."* —Jess Lair

Would you like to have hundreds of sayings, quotes, ideas, principles, or poems memorized that enrich the quality of your thoughts and life, that you could retrieve at any moment without having to refer back to books, files, or documents? Well, I'm going to teach you the technique to memorize any saying and then how to file it in your mind. The technique for doing so is actually a combination of two memory systems, both of which you will learn in the chapters to come. So for now, start compiling some quotes or poems you would like to memorize, and by the end of this book, you will have all the tools necessary to file these quotes away, perform various other types of memory recollection, and understand the numerous other aspects that play a part in allowing you to master your mind.

CHAPTER TWO

Discovering the Doors Dynamic

"When one door closes, another opens; but we often look so long and so regretfully upon the closed door that we do not see the one which has opened for us."

—Alexander Graham Bell

I received my first standing ovation when I was twenty years old. 70,000 people jumped to their feet and gave my performance huge applause. This standing ovation was at Arizona State Sun Devil Stadium. Thousands of Sun Devil fans cheered, whistled, and jumped up and down with joy . . .

. . . Because I was on the *other* team . . .

. . . And I had just missed a field goal.

This pivotal moment in my young life was televised. It felt

like every single person I knew on the planet saw me miss that field goal. This moment was the lowest point of my life. At least, I thought it was.

I was wrong.

Four minutes later, I got my second standing ovation when I missed my second field goal. Again, everyone saw it—along with the televised close-up of me grabbing the kickoff tee and throwing it to the ground in blind fury.

I wish I could go back in time on the sidelines during that game, put my arm around that shattered young man, and say, "Listen, Bob. Cheer up. This isn't the worst thing that will happen to you. There are much worse things to come. You think this is tough? You ain't seen nothing yet!

I was replaced. I would never get that football scholarship I had so depended on to get through college. How could anything be worse than this humiliation? I sank into the deep, dark, slippery, black hole of depression. This was my first real look at that dark, ugly hole.

Have you ever experienced disappointment? How about life-shattering, ego-shredding, mind-consuming disappointment? Well, that's how I felt after I missed those two field goals. A door in my life slammed shut, and I didn't know where to turn next. Let me tell you, some doors have to close in order for new doors to open. It's hard to deal with the disappointment and struggle when a door unexpectedly closes, but the closed door helps you see the bigger, better, brighter door that is soon to swing wide open.

Shortly after I missed those field goals, one of my roommates said, "Come on, Bob, get over it. You've got all kinds of potential. You know what your problem is? You don't dream big enough."

"What do you mean I don't dream big enough?" I retorted.

"I know what you plan on doing after you graduate," he said. "You don't dream big enough."

I looked at him sideways and said, "Oh yeah? Well, what are you going to do after *you* graduate?"

"I'm going to be a multimillionaire."

"Really!" I said. "And how are you going to do that?"

The ridiculous genius of his non-plan was brilliant. Are you ready? He said, "I have no idea *how*, but I'm going to be a multimillionaire." He pointed to a picture of a beautiful home hanging on his wall, one probably cut out of a real estate magazine.

I asked, "Is that your house?"

He said, "Not yet, but it will be."

It *will* be?
Not "it might be"?
Not "I want it to be"?
"It *will* be"?

That simple statement and the matter-of-fact way he said it—wow! It made no sense, in a wonderful, hopeful way. I started to think, dream, plan, *prepare* bigger. Like my roommate, I didn't know *how*, I just knew *what*, and was willing to prepare for the chance to make that dream real.

Years later, my wannabe-millionaire friend decided to invest—in dirt. He bought up large plots of unimproved land and sold them to commercial investors. He is, in fact, now a multimillionaire.

This may have been the first time I recognized that good can come from failure, sometimes in a roundabout way. Had I not failed that day in front of 70,000 cheering (and weeping) fans, I would not have learned that lesson from my wonderful roommate, which created a giant shift in the way I viewed life.

It isn't always, or even usually, about the plan; it's about the preparation.

You want to be lucky? Then prepare and someday your chance will come.

Before I was the college football kicker and missed those two field goals . . .

My high school football team was the best of the best. We were 8–0 my senior year. We weren't just winning, we were winning by large margins—often by more than twenty points a game. The starters were frequently pulled at halftime so as to not run up the score and thereby totally humiliate the opposing team.

I knew I wanted to play football in college, but I didn't exactly know how to make that happen. It was just plain ol' good fortune that the coach from the University of Pittsburg came to watch our high school football team practice. He came specifically to watch three of our linemen—Dave Kaminski, Fred Knoff, and Mark Przybylak (who all went on to be All-Western New York)—and our two amazing twin running backs, Hank and Chuck Goettle. He wasn't looking for kickers, but I didn't know this at the time.

When I realized the coach was there, I decided to take advantage of this opportunity. I teed the ball in the middle of the field and started kicking sixty-yard field goals. He added my name to the list of players he wanted to meet with the next day and asked me to send a film of my kicking to their head coach, but I didn't have any of my game kicks filmed. South Carolina and Alabama were also interested in me and asked me to send them film. I didn't have any film to send them either. Fortunately, my high school coach knew someone at Cortland State in New York, and they offered me a scholarship without having to see film of my kicks. So my initial plan was to attend Cortland State on a football scholarship.

But then I had a dream—yes, I am talking about an actual dream now—that changed everything.

June 26, 1976, a few days after my high school graduation, I woke up from a dream about *Donnie & Marie*, which was rather odd since I had never actually watched Donny and Marie Osmond's show. I had just heard about it because it was a very popular television show at the time. Later that morning, I noticed my sister's *Teen Beat* magazine on the couch. It was the first time I'd even seen a *Teen Beat* magazine. What caught my eye was the word *Osmonds* on the cover. I picked it up and opened it to the cover story. The article mentioned the Osmond brothers' playing football and running track at Brigham Young University. I'd never even heard of Brigham Young University. I looked up BYU's address and sent off a letter to their football office with news clippings of my success as a high school football player.

Why on earth would I do that? All the deadlines were long past due for football players and university admissions at BYU, and I had already committed to Cortland State. But I sent it anyway.

A few weeks later, a letter came back from Norm Chow,

assistant coach, saying they were looking for young men of my caliber. Unfortunately, they could not offer me a scholarship this late in the year, but I was welcome to come on as a walk-on. I would learn later that their sophomore kicker had just announced he was planning on serving a two-year church mission; otherwise, I'm sure they would have ignored my letter. I knew I wouldn't be able to attend without a scholarship, but I went through the interview and application process anyway—I just felt compelled because of that dream—and the football office fast-tracked me to acceptance as a freshman in the fall.

Then the bill from BYU arrived asking for payment.

I still had no money, and my mother wanted nothing to do with my going across the country to Utah to play football on a "maybe," when I had a sure thing at Cortland State. Then Cortland State made a mistake and sent me a bill for tuition and housing. Because we thought I had to pay either way, I talked my mother into helping me my freshman year at BYU so I could earn a scholarship. So, here I come, BYU!

In the first week of August, days before leaving for BYU, I realized how stupid this all was. I was going to a school I had never heard of because of a dream. I headed to the phone to call BYU football and tell them I wasn't coming, but my little sister happened to be on the phone and refused to get off. I went to the living room and turned on the TV. One of the Osmonds was being interviewed on a talk show. I was stunned at the coincidence, and I decided to follow through with my dream and flew off to my new adventure. (By the way, this departure was the first time I'd ever been on an airplane.)

***

Eight months later, I was talking with the BYU football manager, Tom Nibley, during practice, and he asked me if I was going to the football banquet. I replied, tongue in cheek, "No, because my girlfriend is sick and I can't get ahold of Marie Osmond." Although I was clearly joking, he didn't laugh; he simply said, "Ask Jay [Osmond] tomorrow at practice. In fact, go in and ask him right now. He's in the locker room." So I did.

I didn't know it at the time, but this was a huge open door for me. I could have ignored the opportunity or talked myself out of it, but I decided to step over the threshold of this open door, just to see what happened.

I went into the locker room to find Jay. I said something like, "Hey, there's a football banquet... Can you see if Marie would like to go with me?" He actually took my phone number and said he'd get back to me. After he left the locker room, I got dressed to go for a run, but when I was heading down the hall, I spotted Jay again. He had turned around and was walking back toward me. He asked me what I was doing, and I told him I was headed for a run; then he asked if he could come with me. I said sure, and for the rest of the afternoon, we hung out. First, I paced him in a two-mile run, and then we tossed a football around. He called me around seven that night and told me that Marie was busy. Oh well. But...

A month later, I was in a caravan, traveling with the entire Osmond family to the Las Vegas Hilton where Donny and Marie would perform twice a night over the next three weeks. Hanging out in the green room with the Osmonds, I got to meet Michael Jackson; "The Colonel," Elvis Presley's manager; and other celebrities of the '70s.

How did this happen? I simply chose to walk through an open door when presented with an opportunity.

***

During my freshman year, I played on the junior varsity squad. I made only one field goal and missed four. One out of five field goals did not get me the scholarship I needed. I accepted that my football career was done for.

Then something unexpected happened during spring training.

I was on the sideline playing catch with Jay Osmond when I heard my name being called to kick a field goal. I ran out onto the field and looked up quickly at the uprights in the distance. *That goal sure is far away*. There was no time to process that thought. The snap came from the center, and I kicked it right down the middle for a fifty-seven-yard field goal.

I was called in to kick the next field goal a few minutes later. But this time the holder didn't get his hand out from in front of the ball in time, and my kick fluttered off to the left. My own holder had accidentally blocked my kick.

The eyebrows went down. The interest waned. *That great field goal Bob just kicked must have been a fluke.*

The holder, Marc Wilson, felt really bad. It was a mistake. He simply didn't get his hand out from in front of the ball in time. All he could say was an awkward, apologetic "Sorry, Bob." The coaches didn't see what happened. I wasn't called in to kick again, and I didn't get a scholarship. Marc Wilson went on to be an All-American quarterback and played for the Oakland Raiders

I went home to Cheektowaga (Buffalo suburb), New York for a week. Someone there recognized me and asked how football was going. I told him it wasn't going so great. This individual then introduced me to Marv Bateman, the Buffalo Bill's All-Pro kicker and former All-American kicker for the University of Utah. He volunteered to pick me up and take me to Buffalo Bill's Rich Stadium each day that week to help me with my kicking.

I've been asked many times why I help so many without

asking for anything in return. Perhaps it's because people like Marv Bateman didn't ask me for anything in return; he just helped. I wouldn't be where I am today if it weren't for the generosity and kindness of others.

After a couple of minor adjustments, he watched me kick nine fifty-yard field goals in a row. He said in a matter-of-fact way, "You tell your coach that you worked with me and have greatly improved your technique. Tell him he needs to go outside and watch you kick."

Back at school the next week, and filled with new confidence, I marched into Coach Edwards's office and convinced him to watch me kick.

After seeing me kick, Coach agreed that I had improved. He asked if I was currently enrolled to attend that semester. I answered no. I had missed all the deadlines. Coach Edwards reached for the phone, then paused and asked if I had any money for tuition and such. I answered no. He placed a call and arranged to get me back into college with a short-term loan, and just like that, I was back in school and back on the team.

But as the first game approached, Dev Duke was picked to be the starting kicker and I was redshirted.

After spring football, I learned I wasn't going to receive a football scholarship. With no scholarship, I gave up on the idea of playing football. But the following summer, nearing football season, someone on campus said the football office was calling around, trying to contact me. I popped into the office and was whisked right in to see Coach Edwards. He told me that their starting kicker had just been injured waterskiing. Then he asked me if I was willing to come back on the team. I was so excited that I would finally get to live my dream of being a college football kicker.

I helped beat Oregon State, 10–6, with a field goal and extra point.

Then I missed those two field goals against Arizona State and fell from grace.

***

I went back to the JV team and helped beat the number-one-rated junior college in the nation. I nailed every single field goal and extra point for the next three weeks. I walked into Coach Edwards's office and asked if I would get a scholarship if I kicked one hundred percent of all my field goals and extra points the rest of the year.

Coach told me he couldn't do that.

I said, "Well, I don't know how to do better than that, so I quit."

Coach really didn't want to lose his backup, so he promised

me that if I stayed on the team, I would be lettered, get a ring, and get to go to the bowl game. None of that meant anything to me. I needed a scholarship.

Finally, I pointed out that it was obvious my kickoffs went much farther than the starting kicker's. I normally put it in the end zone. Coach agreed. I said, "I'll stay on the team if I can kick all the kickoffs during the home games." Coach agreed, and I was excited again.

Just like in the movie *Rudy*, I called all my family and friends and announced I was the starting kickoff kicker.

The first game was against Texas–El Paso. I was getting ready to go on the field for the kickoff, and he called in the other kicker instead. Rage welled up inside me, but I shoved it down. There would be many opportunities to kick off against Texas–El Paso that day.

I got my chance. I clearly kicked the next three deeper than the other kicker had. But then Coach put the other kicker back in, which triggered me again. And again, I swallowed my anger. I was surprised when he put me in for the final kickoff.

We won, 44–0.

At practice on Monday, Coach walked onto the field and said, "Nice kicking, Robert."

I thanked him and asked if he was going to let me do all the kickoffs that week against Wyoming.

Coach paused and said, “No, I think we’ll do what we did last time.”

I lost my temper. I jerked my helmet off and threw it as far as I could. “I’m out of here! I quit!” (I can see why I wasn’t the starting kicker. A kicker needs to be a bit more stable, calm, and mature.)

The next year, I tried out for the cheerleading squad, and we went on to place sixth nationally. But I was still mad about not being on the football team that year. The starter’s kickoffs still were not reaching the end zone. At halftime, I went onto the field with a few footballs, a kicking tee, and revenge on my mind. I put our mascot, Cosmo, in the end zone and started kicking the footballs over his head and out of the end zone. I was creating quite a stir with the half-time fans. *Why is the cheerleader kicking farther than the team’s kicker?*

I got a request from the football office that week politely asking me to please stop kicking footballs in the stadium during halftime.

My senior year, Coach Edwards invited me back on the team as the backup kicker to Kurt Gunther. I could be the second-team kicker and still be on the cheer squad at the same time. They kept my football equipment in the locker room just in case our starting kicker got hurt.

I ended my troubled athletic career by getting injured doing a double front flip showing off for the crowd and an *NFL Films* television crew.

It was then that the door closed completely on my football days. I had put so much time, commitment, and focus into being a kicker that I didn't know what to do next once that door was closed. But as I said before, when one door closes, another is soon to open up, and it's up to you to take a chance, step over the threshold, and begin a new journey. I had no idea what was in store for me next, but when the door opened, I stepped through.

CHAPTER THREE

A Whole World of Wonderment

"Luck is what happens when preparation meets opportunity."

—Seneca

One day, in a bookstore, I picked up a book on memory improvement and began looking through it. I was mildly interested. As I turned the pages, I became more interested. It seemed I had found something of extreme value. I felt something: a clarity. I didn't yet fully appreciate, or even fully understand, what I was feeling or why, but it was a powerful feeling. A feeling of clarity, like a lightbulb, had just been turned on in my brain. *But why do I feel this way?*

I had already graduated with a bachelor's degree. It was a struggle, but I made it through. I was done with school. I wasn't a college athlete. I wasn't a pro athlete. I certainly wasn't a brilliant student. I was done with all that. *So, what do I need a better memory for?*

If you're anything like me, you probably asked yourself this question before buying this book. You might even be asking yourself this question right now. I can't give a single, defining answer to that question because the reason is different for each individual. But the outcome is the same: memory improvement helps strengthen your mind. And a stronger mind is a limitless supply of life improvement.

But I didn't know that yet. Right then, memory improvement was just an idea that intrigued me, so I bought the book and read it from cover to cover. Everything about this idea of a stronger memory resonated with me. In fact, it seemed to impact my very core. I felt my life being redefined, so I decided to go all in and put it into practice. I was committed to the idea of having a great memory. I studied the illustrations, practiced the exercises, and became increasingly amazed at how much I could remember in just a short amount of time. *Maybe I can be more than average after all.*

As I continued to read and practiced the memory methodology and techniques in the book, I soon became increasingly irritated. *Why has no one ever taught me this stuff before? I should have learned this in junior high.* It was so dang simple! All that struggle through high school and college was easily preventable! I cannot stress that point enough: ALL THE STRUGGLE THROUGH HIGH SCHOOL AND

COLLEGE OR IN YOUR JOB OR JUST IN REMEMBERING EVERYDAY LIFE MATERIAL IS EASILY PREVENTABLE! They should teach memory methodology in every school in the country. No—every school on the planet!

What I was discovering was about more, much more, than just memory; it was about mind mastery and mental prowess. It was the key to success in so many ways, and I was mastering it. My confidence skyrocketed. I began to understand how it felt to be truly smart. For the first time in my life, I believed that I could learn just about anything. This realization was life altering. I'd gone from being mediocre to being a maestro of memory.

***

When human beings discover something of value, our instinct is not to keep it to ourselves; our instinct is to share it with others, anybody and everybody—family, friends, neighbors, even strangers. I was so excited that I started teaching this technique to almost everyone I met. I could be anywhere, talking with anyone, and I'd say something like, "Hey, I gotta show you something. Here, list twenty objects on this piece a paper; number them; and by the time you've finished writing them down, I'll be able to repeat them back to you, in order. For example, you might write, '#1 horse, #2 penguin, #3 truck.' Got it? Okay, go."

These situations became funny. People would start writing

a list down and not say a word. I'd interrupt, "C'mon, I'm a memory master, not a mystic. I can't read your mind; you gotta say the objects and their numbers out loud while you are writing them down so I know what you are writing, so I can remember it. Then I'll show you how I do it."

After they completed their list of twenty items, I'd say, "Pick any number, and I'll tell you the object that goes with it." I would not only identify that object and the next they'd call out, but the entire list of twenty items they had written on that page, and I could do it in any order they chose—forward, backward, from the middle outward, and any other order they threw at me.

It worked. It *always* worked. It was impressive. It was fun. It was simple. And, with a little practice, it was easy. They were first astounded. Then they were intrigued.

Are you ready to know how I did it?

I used a memory technique called the Linking System. In fact, this was the first memory technique I ever learned. The Linking System is a simple memory technique consisting of only two steps. First, create a visual image for each item on the list (remember, vivid detail is most important). Second, create a vivid interaction between two consecutive images on the list. Each item on the list is connected to the item before it and to the item following it, just like a link in a chain.

In other words, you produce a brief motion picture in your mind with only two items in each scene. Move from one scene to the other with clear focus on each imagined scene. If you let your mind wander from one of the scenes, you may miss a link in the memory chain. If you skip over a mental image because you think it is too simple or too silly, you limit your ability to memorize. I've seen a four-year-old memorize fifty items on her first try using the Linking System.

Ready? Okay. I'm going to tell you a list of objects. All you have to do is imagine them two at a time; the first item actively interacting with the second, the second with the third, and so on. This is how you can easily commit a list to memory.

The first object to remember is a bonnet. Visualize picking up a bonnet. What color is it? Say *bonnet* out loud.

After *bonnet* is *giraffe*. Visualize the giraffe. See what it looks like. Now see yourself tie a bonnet to the giraffe's head. Say *giraffe* out loud.

Next is *telephone booth*. Remember what those are? See it in your mind's eye. Now see a giraffe stuck in a telephone booth. Say *telephone booth*.

Next is *steamroller*. See the steamroller. Visualize a telephone booth getting ran over and crushed by that steamroller. Don't worry about the giraffe, he's okay. Say *steamroller*.

Next, I want you to remember *boat*. Visualize a steamroller rolling into the water and becoming a boat. Say *boat*.

After boat is *snake*. Visualize hundreds of snakes chasing you on the boat. What kind of snakes are they? Anacondas? Rattlesnakes? Little green garden snakes? Say *snake* out loud.

After snake is *professor*. Visualize a professor in college who looks like a snake. Say *professor*.

Next is *soup*. Picture a professor in the bottom of a bowl of soup.

After soup is *airplane*. Visualize the bowl of soup again and an airplane landing in your soup.

After airplane is *elephant*. Visualize an elephant flying through the sky like an airplane.

After elephant is *tree*. Visualize an elephant climbing a tree.

Next, I want you to remember *moon*. See trees covering the moon.

After moon is *bathtub*. Visualize the moon taking a bath in your bathtub.

After bathtub is *motorcycle.* Visualize a bathtub-motorcycle going down the street.

The last item to remember is *ice cream.* Visualize motorcycles in an ice cream cone.

Now, with these images linked in your mind, start with *bonnet* and see how many of the items you can remember. If you can't remember one of the items, relax and let the mental picture float into your mind. Don't worry, it will work. You didn't lose the picture; you've just misplaced it. Where did you put it? It is right after the preceding picture and just before the next one. It's there.

Focus on the associations, and write down the fifteen items.

1.
2.
3.
4.
5.
6.
7.
8.
9.
10.
11.
12.
13.
14.
15.

Well, how did you do? If you missed a link, your mind may have wandered when you were visualizing it and connecting it to the next thing on the list. Revisualize the weak link. The revisualized link will then become the strongest link on the whole list. Now give it one more try.

There! I bet you named all fifteen this time! Like anything else, this will get easier and easier as you practice it.

Here is another list to practice memorizing. Perhaps this is a list of things you need to pick up at the supermarket. Visualize each item, and use the Linking System to link the items together.

APPLES
CHICKEN
MUSHROOM
SOUP
FLOOR
WAX
TOOTHPASTE
BREAD
DEODORANT
ICE CREAM
HOT DOGS
BROCCOLI
DOG FOOD
HAIR GEL

PEANUT
BUTTER
TALCUM POWDER
EGGS

Notice how much easier it is getting already? Remember, go slow and steady, visualize each item, and then link it.

Now that you've learned the Linking System, you can apply it to more important matters, like if you have to remember a big list of items for a test, or a list of steps for something at work, or if you have to remember twenty ingredients for a recipe, or if you just want to impress your friends and family. You now know how to apply this system to any kind of list!

***

Dave was a pre-med student. After teaching him how to master this memory technique and several others, he earned perfect scores on all of his pathophysiology tests. His professor called Dave into his office and told him that the highest grade below his was in the 60s. Dave had blown the curve. The professor had never seen anyone do what Dave had done. Convinced that Dave had cheated, he quizzed him in detail to see whether he really knew the material. Dave did. Now convinced that Dave was a genius, the professor offered to write him a letter of recommendation to any medical school in the country.

The next person I taught this memorization system to was my brother, Tom. He was an army private stationed in Killeen, Texas. A few months after learning the process, he told me that he had won the Soldier of the Month competition. The competition was based on their knowledge of the Army Manual, which was a thick book containing all kinds of facts, like the velocity and range of different types of ammunition. Many of those he competed with for Soldier of the Month had been in the army for over a decade. But Tom won. He said it was easy. He said he basically memorized the entire manual using the techniques I had shared with him.

At this time, I was still living in my college town. While on a run with two of my former university professors, I shared with them—actually taught them on the fly, as it were—some of the basic techniques. They told me that I needed to go back to college and get a master's degree, perhaps in communications. They both thought I would be an excellent teacher or trainer.

That spoke to me, but could I pull it off? I had struggled as an undergraduate, and, quite frankly, I felt lucky to have even graduated. I had spent countless hours in the library to pull off a 3.0 GPA and had decided for certain to never go back. But they opened the door, I stepped through, and back to school I went.

The next time someone tells you there's no such thing as luck, be bold and say, "Actually there is." And then when they look at you funny and tell you to explain, you can proudly proclaim, “Luck is when preparation meets opportunity.” When I started reading and studying memory techniques, I had no idea what I was preparing for, but it was preparation nonetheless. And because of this preparation, a whole world of opportunities was about to come my way.

CHAPTER FOUR

The Remarkable Rippling Reaction

"Progress always involves risk. You can't steal second base and keep your foot on first."

—Frederick B. Wilcox

There is one more component to luck that you should know, and it is the most important component. You are well prepared, and a great opportunity has just arrived. What do you do next? Take action! Don't ignore an opportunity or talk yourself out of going for it. Take action and watch how doors just continue to swing wide open because of your boldness.

Because I was prepared with memory training techniques and shared them with some of my former professors on a run, they gave me the opportunity to go back to college for my master's degree, and I took action. I chose to listen to them and went back to school. I had no idea how many doors would open up because of this action.

It was time to put my memory training to actual use. Remembering a bonnet on a giraffe in a phone booth is one thing, but what about college-level material? Would my memory techniques still work?

The professor began his first lecture by bragging that, in sixteen years, no one had ever achieved a perfect score on any of his fifty-question multiple-choice tests. I'm not sure if he was trying to inspire us or discourage us. I wanted to raise my hand and ask, "Have you ever considered that maybe you just can't teach?" but I decided not to.

The first exam approached. It was to be held in the testing center, a special room in the campus library dedicated to administering and scoring tests. Students would submit their student ID to check in. Then they would check out when they had completed their examination. The facilitator's computer would immediately score the test and record the time it had taken to complete the exam. I completed the process in twenty-seven minutes, scoring 100%—the first perfect score ever in this professor's class.

He gave me a zero for cheating and threatened to flunk me. "There's no way you could get a perfect score, especially in such a short period of time," he told me. He said that the average time to take the test was about an hour, and I had done it in less than half an hour. And the next highest score to mine was in the 80s; therefore, my professor thought that I must have cheated.

I felt a surge of something I had never before felt in academics—not anger, not even resistance. I felt confidence. I challenged him.

I pushed back playfully with, "Just for fun, why don't you ask me anything from the four chapters we were just tested on?"

The professor grabbed his book.

Wait! He wrote the book, so why does he have to refer to it?

He opened it at random, flipped through a few pages, and asked, "What are the fourteen attributes of a grapevine in communications?"

First, I told him the page number where the fourteen attributes were listed. Then, I named all fourteen attributes in the order they appeared on that page. He was dumbfounded.

I don't know if you've ever had a chance to throw a dart at a puffed-up professor, but this was my moment, and I am embarrassed to say that it was fun!

To his credit, he relented and gave me the perfect score I had earned. He did more than that. He began to believe that I was actually smart. It was a pivotal event. I could see my life changing right before my eyes. *I began to believe I could do anything.*

As I created new ways to organize and retain information, my GPA jumped from an undergraduate 3.0 to a grad school 3.8, and I soon earned my first perfect 4.0 semester. This was truly amazing. I could hardly believe what had happened. My educational experience transformed from one of futility and drudgery into an exciting, fulfilling adventure.

I felt the urge to help as many students as I possibly could by showing them my memory techniques. So I started sharing my techniques with groups of students. I'd ask, "Would you like to spend less time studying, have more free time, and have more fun?" Then I'd demonstrate the skill and tell them how easy it was to learn. "I can teach you how to memorize terms, definitions, formulas, equations, names, and faces—anything you need to remember to succeed in school—like the person's name you're on a date with!"

What I didn't realize at the time was not only could they spend less time studying and have more fun, but the studying itself was transformed into fun. Learning in a group was a blast, and using the memory techniques made it even better! More than that, it was *gratifying*. It was wonderful to make a difference in the lives of so many students. I watched myself evolve from being a struggling student to having a position of influence where I could help my peers succeed in school and in life. It was especially rewarding to hear about them spreading the word by helping other students and then, later on, helping employees, associates, friends, and especially their children, who were just beginning their educational adventure. This was such a profound life-changing experience, I wanted to do more.

So, one day, I walked into my directing professor's office with a proposal. For a special-project elective, I would develop and promote a two-hour class designed to train 200 students how to enhance their memories, strengthen their minds, and make studying fun. My professor thought that would certainly be worth three credit hours toward my master's degree. How exciting! I put together the materials and prepared a free lecture. A classroom on campus was scheduled. Now all I needed was to find a way to get students to show up.

I remembered the anatomy class I had failed twice in undergrad before finally managing to achieve a C. I asked my old anatomy professor if I could have five minutes in his class to promote my free memory training. Surprisingly, he agreed.

Sometimes success is just that simple. Don't just think about it, do it. Take action!

He allowed me to give a brief demonstration in his class the next day to promote my seminar. Not only did a couple hundred of his students attend my seminar, but the professor himself showed up.

About a third of the way through the training, I asked the students to get a partner and practice the memory techniques together. As I watched them pair up, something amazing unfolded. They were smiling, laughing, and filled with delight as they realized that they were having a lightbulb moment. They were having fun—and feeling smarter by the minute! It was amazing!

That deeper, more profound feeling washed over me again. I was making a difference. I could see it happen in real time, right there before my eyes. Wow. It was life changing, for them—and for me. Overwhelmed, I stepped into the hall and stood there for a few moments to regain my composure.

Imagine discovering you can hold a couple hundred students' attention; have them laughin' and learnin' and reacting with amazement and joy as they realize the power and potential they have always had but were never aware of until this moment. It reminded me of the first time I actually kicked a football out of the end zone. I was shocked with amazement. *How did that happen?*

My composure regained, I stepped back into the lecture hall.

Two weeks later, the professor called. He told me that I had created a problem. He taught three large sections of anatomy and graded on a curve. The class I taught my memory techniques to had blown the curve. But there was a solution: the students in the other two classes found out about the special training and wanted the same advantage. Would I teach them as well? The professor who had essentially flunked me a couple years earlier was actually asking me to teach the rest of his students. Wow.

The great Zig Ziglar believed that one way to get experience, especially when no one will hire you, is to do it for free. That is, in fact, how he got started as a world-class speaker. So that's what I did. I went all over campus demonstrating, organizing, and conducting seminars in memory improvement. I trained over 3,000 college students—and I did it for free.

I gained even more experience by setting up a regular time, once every week, to meet with students who had questions on how to apply these memory techniques to specific classes—geology, philosophy, psychology, math, languages, the arts...The list was endless. Over the next year, I created special memory systems to help students mentally store and quickly and accurately retrieve information in dozens of subjects. I created special techniques for memorizing rocks and minerals, artwork by the artist, music by the composer, constellations in astronomy, and origins and insertions in anatomy. What a thrill to help med students with pathology and pharmacology; law students gain an exquisite command of case law; master's students with their theses and preparation for their oral exams; and PhD candidates defend their dissertations.

I taught so many students so much smarter than me and helped them change their lives. The rippling effect began and would continue to stretch out until . . . well . . . forever.

***

How exciting it was to create new memory techniques that could be applied across multiple subjects. It was soul-satisfying to make a significant difference in the lives of others.

During the last semester of my master's program, I walked into class—walked in late, I should note—in sweats, a t-shirt, and flip-flops, with a large Diet Coke in hand. My late arrival interrupted our class's guest speaker, Bruno Vassal, Avon World Headquarters' Corporate Director of Training and Management Development. As I casually took my seat and listened to our guest speaker, something occurred to me:

Is this an opportunity? What if I talked to him about using my memory training for his company? Would he take me seriously? Why not try? I was used to trying. He might reject me. I was used to that too. So . . .

I walked up to him after class, resplendent in my t-shirt and flip-flops. "You guys could really use some memory training. You should fly me to New York to train the Avon staff. Your representatives need to remember products and costs, what's new and coming, and they especially need to remember the names of the people they're dealing with."

It was a bold move.

Bruno glanced over at me. "Send a proposal."

So I did. I mailed my proposal to him the next day. There were three options:

Option one ~ $1,000 dollars a day, airfare, hotel, and buy me dinner at a great NY Italian restaurant.

Option two ~ Airfare, hotel, and buy me dinner at a great NY Italian restaurant.

Option three ~ Just buy me dinner at a great NY Italian restaurant.

I could figure out how to get there on my own. I didn't want to lose this opportunity over the cost of a plane ticket.

A couple of weeks later, my directing professor called me into his office. He told me he had received a call from Bruno at Avon. Bruno wanted to know if I was for real. My professor assured him that I was and recommended me highly.

To my astonishment, Bruno agreed to Option 1. In 1985 a

thousand dollars was a lot of money for a college student. February 12, 1985, I flew to New York for my first "business trip." The next day, I taught Avon's corporate training directors techniques for how to remember products, prices, and all kinds of other company info.

Then we had dinner at a great NY Italian restaurant.

On my final day in New York, Bruno stunned me with an offer to work at Avon headquarters after I graduated. It was a great opportunity. *Working in New York with a major name like Avon? That would be huge!*

But I felt that my memory training needed to be shared with more people than just the Avon staff. My memory training needed to be shared with anyone and everyone who would listen, so I decided not to go to work with Avon, and instead decided to see where my memory techniques would take me next. But Bruno still gave me a letter of recommendation on Avon letterhead declaring my abilities and the value of memory training for Avon. He signed it with his title of Head Corporate Training Director, Avon World Headquarters. I still have this letter today.

I was invigorated after my time at Avon and learned that taking action has its benefits, so I decided to keep it up, to keep looking for opportunities to take action and spread my memory training.

I approached my college football coach, LaVell Edwards, about training the team with my memory skills. The players had to memorize plays, of course; and, even more important, they needed to get good grades. So memory training made perfect sense for them.

As part of my sales pitch to impress Coach Edwards, I memorized a random page out of the phone book. This was 1985 when phone books were big! We didn't have Siri on our cell phones—heck, we didn't have cell phones.

"Coach, I memorized 400 phone numbers and 400 names just to prove that my techniques work." I handed him the page. "Try me."

He told me a name. I told him the phone number. He told me another name. I told him the phone number. We did this several times. Then I switched it up.

"Now, Coach, just for fun, tell me a phone number off that page, and I'll tell you the name that goes with it."

I answered him correctly each time.

Coach Edwards said, "Wow, Robert. I'm impressed by your intellectual acumen in this area."

I said, "Thanks, Coach—I think. What's *acumen* mean?"

He laughed. And I got the job.

Not only did I get to train the team, but after a few weeks, I got another testimonial letter from a Division I football team. I added this letter to what was becoming my portfolio of major recommendations. These letters gave me the credibility I needed to move forward in my upcoming speaking and training career.

By the time I graduated with my master's degree, I had brand-new discoveries about retention and recall and solid experience as an effective presenter. I was ready for the next step. Or the next leap. I was prepared, opportunities were coming, and I was ready to take action.

CHAPTER FIVE

The Sweet Sound of Success

"The problem with not having a goal is that you can spend your whole life running up and down the field and never score."

—Bill Copeland

Things were falling into place, and my memory training was taking off. But I want to pause and make one thing crystal clear: I had a resume of failures to get to this point.

In high school, I had a goal to be the halfback on the football team. But it turned out I was too slow. So, no to that goal.

Okay, I could be the fullback. That didn't work out either. Another failure.

Wide Receiver? Nope. Failure.

Okay, how about a distance runner? *Surely, I can accomplish that, right?* On the first day, with the first workout, there was freezing rain. I lasted three minutes. Another failure.

How about pole vault? *Pole vaulting isn't that popular. I bet I could train really hard and become the state record holder!* I never came close to the state record. Okay, how about the Western New York record? Nope. County record? Negative. More failure.

At this point, I decided to start setting goals in something other than athletics. *How about my social life?* I set a goal to get a really nice, attractive girl to go out with me.

Joni?

"No, thank you."

Vivian?

"Nope."

Ruby?

"You're really nice, Bob, but no."

Marie?

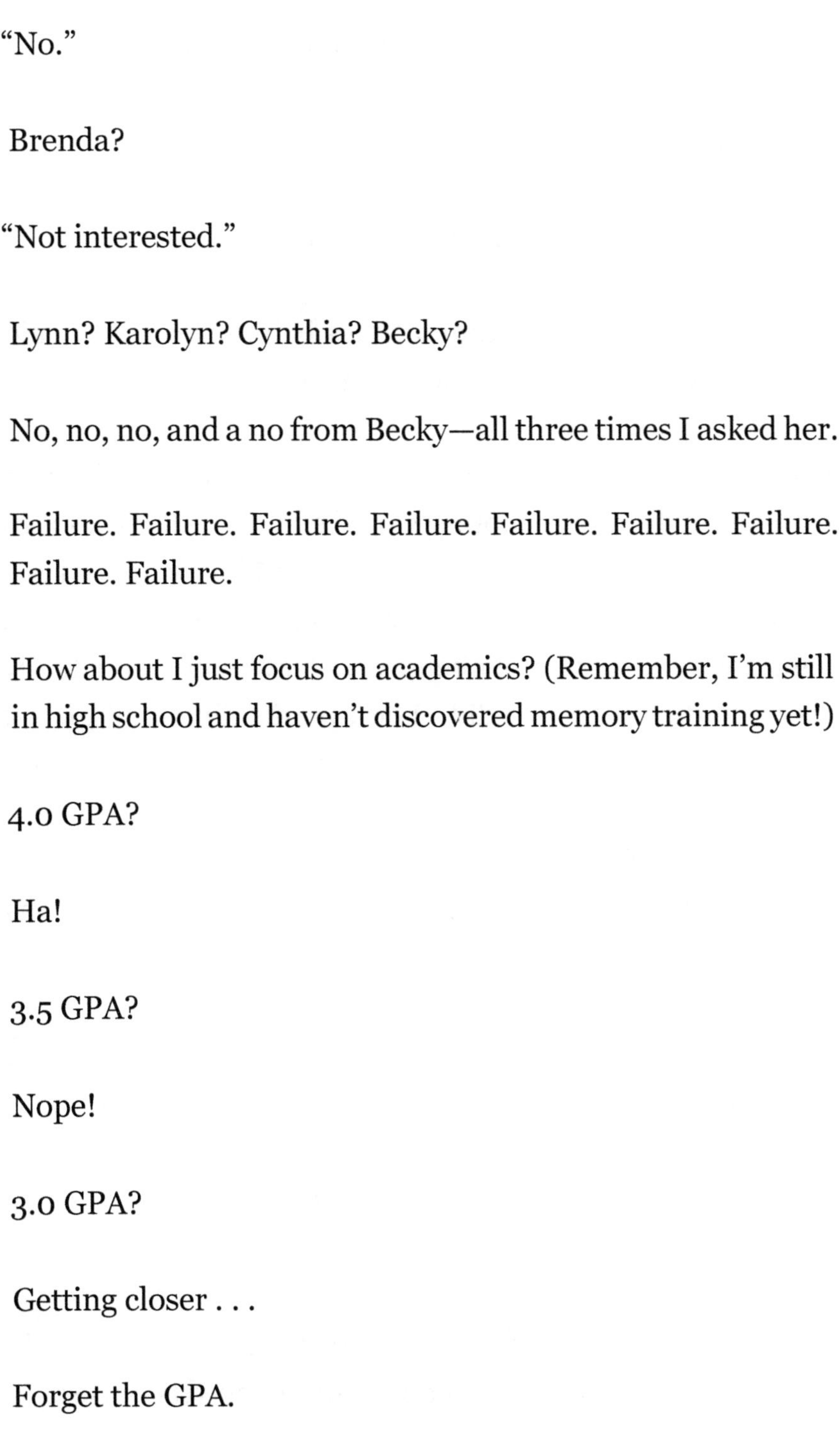

"No."

Brenda?

"Not interested."

Lynn? Karolyn? Cynthia? Becky?

No, no, no, and a no from Becky—all three times I asked her.

Failure. Failure. Failure. Failure. Failure. Failure. Failure. Failure. Failure.

How about I just focus on academics? (Remember, I'm still in high school and haven't discovered memory training yet!)

4.0 GPA?

Ha!

3.5 GPA?

Nope!

3.0 GPA?

Getting closer . . .

Forget the GPA.

I once asked a young lady to marry me. She said no.

I asked her again. She said no again.

I kept on asking. She kept on saying no.

She turned me down a dozen times before she finally said yes. Yippee! Then she said no again. Why?

Every time I asked her to marry me, she would discuss it with her mother. Her mother would say, "You don't want to marry him. You don't love him. He doesn't love you. And you know what? Bob's not very smart. What do you mean he has a master's degree? I don't believe it. Have you ever actually seen the diploma? You did? You saw his diploma? I don't believe it. Call the university. You can fake those things, you know."

Every goal I set seemed to be a failure. At least I was consistent.

When I told this story at a leadership retreat in Colorado Springs for the Denver Broncos, one of the players commented about my path of failure:

". . . And you're a motivational speaker?"

I answered, "Although failure might have been my outcome in so many circumstances, other doors were opened because of it."

I had the goal of being the halfback on the football team. It didn't work out. However, the coach said, "I need a kicker. Let's see who can kick." I did not know I could kick—certainly not farther than anyone else on the team. But I could and I did. And that got me on a Division I football team.

I had the goal of getting a scholarship. That didn't work out for me either, but it kept me in college, where I earned a bachelor's degree from a major university. And that later made it possible for me to begin my master's program, where I then helped thousands of college students with memory training.

I had the goal of being the starting kicker because the backup kicker didn't get to travel with the team to the away games. But even as the backup kicker, I figured out how to travel to the away games. I tried out for the cheerleading squad, remember? And I made it. Our cheer squad placed sixth nationally. I was blessed with so many opportunities that never would have occurred if I had given up after my first failure of not becoming the fullback.

In 1983, two years after I graduated with my bachelor's degree, I decided to try out for pro football—despite the fact that I had played in only three varsity college games. I was told, "You're crazy. You can't do that. It can't be done."

I learned that when you have a dream you have to be careful whom you share it with. I also learned to choose better friends. Negative people can impact your life, even when you don't know they are doing it. I also learned that they were right. Crap. But something happened on the way to failure.

When I was thinking of trying out for pro football, I wisely decided to run it by an older, wiser mentor, a friend who had succeeded in business, Rick Farr, PhD, an entrepreneurial genius.

"Yeah, go for it, Bob. You can't lose."

"What do you mean I can't lose? I'm good at that."

"Look, Bob, there are two attributes of every successful person who ever walked the face of the earth: they were all persistent . . . and they all failed."

"What? That's the key to success? Failure?"

"Yes, sorta. Do you know how many people think failure is a bad thing? It isn't. It's your failures that teach you how to be successful. Go fail as fast as you can, because guess what is right on the other side of failure? Success."

He continued, "If you try out for pro football *and fail*—fantastic! You will learn great things that will help you the rest of your life." Then he asked another profound question: "And what if you try out and *succeed* and make lots of money and become famous? Fantastic! You're young; *you'll fail later.* You should be okay."

The key was to prepare. "It is better to be prepared for an opportunity and not have one than to have an opportunity and not be prepared." —Whitney M. Young Jr.

So I prepared. I could not guarantee success, but I could guarantee being prepared.

Every day, I kicked one hundred footballs—I mean five footballs twenty times—and a kid would shag them. His motivation? As I said before, there was no pressure here, and pressure is inherent in field goal kicking, so I invented pressure. Once, randomly, within every five field goal attempts, he would holler, "This is it!" If I missed that attempt, I'd have to pay him ten bucks. Pressure is part of the game of football. (I used to think it was also a part of life. More on that later.)

Every day, I ran eight to ten miles, lifted weights, and ran the stairs. Every day, in every way, I did everything I knew how to do to be physically and mentally prepared for this opportunity. Remember the quotation? My mantra? "I will prepare and someday my chance will come." I fulfilled the quotation beautifully. I was fully prepared to play pro football. But no opportunity came by. No one would even let me try out. Why? I needed an agent. Not many pro football agents want to represent former college cheerleaders. It was a lost cause. My opportunity to succeed was never going to come. Again I was wrong. It did come.

If you work hard toward a dream and run into a closed door, there is a very good chance that someone will appear, as if out of nowhere, often someone you don't even know, who will open the door for you.

A former teammate who was headed for the NFL saw how hard I was working toward *my* goal and gave me the number of his agent. I called every day for two weeks. I left messages on his answering machine. He wouldn't return my calls. Finally, one day, a lady answered the phone. With great enthusiasm and excitement, I almost yelled into the phone, "Is Greg Bloom there?"

She said no.

"Well . . . do you have his home phone number?"

She hesitated. "Um . . . Who is this again?"

"I'm Bob Kittell. I'm a kicker, and I'm really good. He's going to want to see me kick." I don't remember what else I said, but I'm sure my enthusiasm overwhelmed her.

After a pause, she said (probably to get rid of me), "Okay, okay, here's his number. By the way, who told you to call me to get his number?"

"Well, this is his office number, isn't it?"

She said, "Honey, you misdialed. You called my home number, but he just happens to be a friend of the family." The heavens were opening to make sure I played pro football. I was certain of it.

I called the agent, and he agreed to watch me kick. He was pretty excited until the teams he called to get references on me started calling him back, telling him they contacted Brigham Young University sports information and found out I only played in three varsity games and ended up a cheerleader. He was sorry, but there was nothing more he could do.

I kept practicing anyway.

Two weeks later, another player ran into me on campus and told me the Denver coach was in our football office visiting with some of our players.

I had hurt my knee the night before, but this was my shot, and I wasn't going to let it slip by. I jumped on my motorcycle and headed for the football offices. The coach was in the far corner surrounded by some of our team's superstars.

Standing by the door (so they wouldn't see me limp across the floor) and with unparalleled enthusiasm and great spirit, and with what I was sure was an engaging power of command, I shouted, "Hey, you guys looking for a kicker?"

The players turned and stared at me as if I was out of my mind. The coach smiled. "Well, we already signed four kickers for camp this year."

With the ignorance born of great, if misplaced, enthusiasm, I replied, "Great! What would it take to sign a *fifth* kicker?"

"Well, he'd have to be pretty darn good."

"Coach, look out the window. You see that field goal post out there? I'll kick a forty-yard field goal that will clear the uprights, go over the fence, and hit the cars. Then I'll do a kickoff. It will go right through the back of the end zone." I paused and looked him dead in the eye. "That's *pretty darn good*, isn't it?"

Looking somewhat amused, he checked his watch and said, "Okay, I'll see you at two o'clock. I'll give you fifteen minutes."

I ended up kicking fifteen consecutive field goals, starting from a distance of twenty yards and advancing in ten-yard increments to sixty yards. I nailed every one of them. (Granted, this is a lot easier when you don't have a 300-pound lineman rushing you, with death and destruction on his mind.)

The coach was so impressed, he signed me on the spot, and

I went to camp. "This is great!" Can you guess what happened next?

On the third day, I was cut. I never played a day of pro football. Crap.

Once, after telling this apparently uninspiring story to a friend, he said, "Why did you tell me this stupid story? Now I'm depressed!"

I replied, "So you think I just wasted eight months of my life preparing for nothing?"

"Yeah, it sure seems like a waste of time—a colossal waste of time."

"But was it?"

"Well . . . yes, I guess . . . I think so . . . What do you mean?"

By trying something others said I could never accomplish, something that appeared at the end to be a colossal waste of time, I got to the top of a mountain I never would have—and arguably never should have—even attempted to climb. But there, on top of that mountain, standing for a moment on a summit people said I could never reach, I could see things I could never ever see before.

I often remember this quotation from Zig Ziglar: "What you

get by reaching your goal isn't nearly as important as what you become by reaching for it." This quotation has certainly been proven true in my life. I wouldn't be where I am today if it weren't for my failures and where my failures led me. Success could be just a few failures away!

***

Soon after graduating with my master's degree—something I never could have done without my memory system—I began thinking of all the students I had helped—for free. I asked my friend Nick Muir, an accomplished entrepreneur, if he thought students would pay for this. Nick thought they would and suggested trying to sell it door to door. I was skeptical at first. I mean, really? Door to door? But then I remembered a story a young lady told me about how she got started in her sales profession.

When she was little, she put up a lemonade stand. No one came to buy lemonade, and she wondered, "Where are all the people?" It occurred to her that the people were behind the doors, so she changed strategies. Instead of waiting for customers to come to her, she decided to go find them. She went down the street selling her lemonade door to door. And it worked.

Her mother came out wondering where her little girl was and found her down the street pouring lemonade for a neighbor. Her mother said, "Honey, what are you doing?"

The little girl turned to her mother, her eyes filled with the excitement and wonder of discovery, and she said, "Mom, the money is behind the doors!"

Great story, but I was still reluctant about door-to-door sales. I didn't see how that could work with a two-hour memory course. I told Nick I probably wouldn't do it. Nick said, "Hang on, I'll be right there." In a few minutes Nick was at my door. He took me to a copy center and helped me create tickets to my seminar. We printed a couple hundred coupons.

"Now, drive up to the junior college, and go door to door with this. Just give it a shot."

So I tried it. I started selling my memory seminar to students door to door for twenty bucks—five dollars for the ticket, fifteen dollars at the door. I focused on off-campus student housing. I would present to half a dozen students at a time, convincing over half of them to attend my "two-hour money-back-guaranteed memory seminar."

It worked. This was exciting! I made more money in an hour working for myself than I'd ever made in a month working for someone else.

After three weeks of wonderful success, it was time to expand our horizon. I bought a van, convinced two of my friends to come with me, and headed to Arizona State to try my memory training on that campus. We called our company Memory Improvement Systems.

Unfortunately, these four-year university students were not as willing to let you into their apartment to do a presentation as the two-year junior college students were. I was suddenly discouraged at my failure. I had already purchased a van and equipment, so we headed for Utah State University to give it another try.

We split up the area and started knocking on doors. After about an hour, one of my salesmen found me and excitedly told me that forty guys in a thing called a "fraternity" were waiting for me to do a demonstration. I hadn't seen *Animal House* yet, so I didn't know what a fraternity was. But I soon found out.

Out of the forty guys I gave the presentation to, thirty of them signed up for the seminar.

I asked, "Are there any more of these houses full of students?"

They laughed. "Yes, lots of them."

"Really? Seriously? You've got to be kidding me! How many universities have them?"

Thus began our nationwide tour of over a hundred major universities across the United States. I was making more money than I had ever imagined I could. Then I messed up.

A guy walked up to me at my wedding reception and said, "I see what you're doing with memory and students. You need to get this information on TV."

This was 1986, the beginning of the infomercial era. Back then it was relatively inexpensive to advertise on television.

He said, "Bob, you'll be the first person advertising memory techniques on television. It will go big. I know it will. I can help you."

I was the student, and the teacher had appeared. The door had just swung wide open, and guess what? I didn't do it. I didn't step across the threshold. Is there such a thing as a missed opportunity? I learned there isn't. Someone always picks up the ones you leave behind. I turned my back on what turned out to be a tremendous opportunity—for someone else.

Some guy with a system called Mega Memory took the nation by storm shortly after I turned down the TV offer. He had picked up the opportunity that I left behind. The worst part was that my material was significantly more advanced. And my credentials were superior: I had trained the Avon staff, the BYU football team, thousands of students in groups, and many others, one on one. It didn't matter that my course was superior or that my credentials were superior. I didn't take action and he did.

I promised myself that, from that time forward, when a door opened I would step through. And I have. Sometimes it wasn't the door for me, but that was alright because at least I didn't have to wonder about that door anymore. Sometimes the door led to a dead end, and that was also good to know. But often, the door opened to amazing opportunities, experiences, and people. In any case, taking action always led to something a whole lot more valuable than doing nothing.

I considered this missed opportunity to be one of my biggest failures: failure to act. But I didn't let it stop me. I kept pressing forward, and what was in store for me was so much bigger than this failure.

CHAPTER SIX

Relationship Gains by Remembering Names

"The sweetest sound to an individual's ear is the sound of their own name."

—Dale Carnegie

Let me go back to the first day of my master's program.

The first day of winter semester, our professor asked everyone to stand, state their name, and tell the class their favorite moment during the vacation break. I thought this would be a great time to practice one of my memory techniques. After all forty of my classmates finished introducing themselves, my professor said, "If anyone can come up here right now and tell me everyone's name, I'll give you an A for the class."

I was stunned. I was using my memory technique just for fun, but here was an opportunity to secure an A on the first day. I jumped up and volunteered. "I can! I can!" I amazed everyone as I recalled everyone's name in the class. I had one little hesitation that kept everyone on the edge of their seats . . .

There was one individual that I couldn't remember, so I asked him to turn his head around and look at the back wall. Everyone thought I was nuts. But I instantly said "Ryan" as soon as I saw the back of his head, and I was correct. Since I was seated behind him, I had used my memory technique on the back of his head instead of using his face.

I got the A.

So, would you like to know how I did it? Would you like to learn how to remember the name of everybody you meet? Well, I'll tell you. But first, let me tell you why it's important to remember someone's name, why it's important to remember the name of everyone you ever come into contact with.

Most people have trouble remembering someone's name. You run into someone and say, "Hey, I recognize your face, but I forgot your name." But I bet the opposite has never happened: "Bill! How are you doing? I remember your name; it's your face I forgot."

Remembering someone's name is one of the most important and basic parts in building rapport. In fact, it's one of the greatest compliments you can give a person. After all, it's not what you know, it's who you know. But in order to *know* them and build a relationship with them, you first have to remember their name.

This principle is especially important in business. There are three reasons people typically get involved with you in business. Money is number three. That's right, money is not number one! The second reason is trust. And the number-one reason people want to do business with you is simply because they like you. And the first step for someone to like you is to remember their name.

Let's say you met someone named John at a business meeting, a networking group, or just at a social event. A couple of days go by, and here comes John walking down the street toward you. You mentally scramble to remember his name, but resort to "Hey pal, how are ya?" Problem number one: John knows you don't know his name. Problem number two: you know that John knows that you don't know his name. You're already off on the wrong foot, and you feel uncomfortable. It would have been so much easier if you just had remembered John's name.

One method to help you remember someone's name is to repeat it back to them and make sure you have the correct pronunciation. If this person is a potential client or business partner, ask them to confirm the spelling of their name, which will eliminate any errors in future correspondence or emails. It may seem a little overboard but most individuals will appreciate the effort because their name is important to them. After you've learned their name, use it often in the conversation, not only to assure them that you are paying attention but also to help you remember it.

But I told you I'd share my advanced memory technique on how to remember names. When I remembered all forty of my classmates' names on the first day, I used a system called the Image Method. Our brains are designed to remember images best. A person's face is an image, which, again, is why we remember faces but not names. So the Image Method uses the person's face to help you remember that person's name. Here's how it works:

When someone tells you their name and you repeat it back to them to clarify and ask for spelling if it is unusual, the first step in the Image Method is to convert their name into a picture. Let's take our friend John from earlier. John has just introduced himself. The word John, in modern vernacular, is a toilet. (You obviously wouldn't share the fact that you are using a toilet to remember John's name.)

The second step is to pick out a prominent physical feature about the person. John has a large, square chin. (Again, you don't comment on their physical feature out loud; this is all happening inside your mind.)

The third step is to link the image from step one with the physical feature from step two. For John, you would visualize a miniature toilet perched on his square chin. With an image like that, it will be hard to forget John's name.

Now let's try this method with Ann Spears. Ann has vibrant blue eyes. Visualize a Raggedy Ann doll jumping out of her left eye. Then imagine Raggedy Ann throwing little spears.

Using this method definitely takes some creativity, but it can be fun! This method is how I was able to remember all forty of my classmates' names on the first day. The reason I had to have Ryan turn his head around was because, when I was sitting behind him, I linked the hairs on the back of his neck to rye bread. I visualized the hairs growing rapidly into rye bread before my eyes. And, hey, it worked and I secured an A in that class on the first day!

Here's a quick memory exercise to help you remember names:

This is Mark. Say out loud "Hi, Mark." Visually pick up a marking pen. Mark has a big nose. Visually shove the marking pen up Mark's nose.

This is Scott. "Hi, Scott." Tape Scott's beard with Scotch (for Scott) tape and yank it off his beard. That should be memorable.

This is Irene. “Hi, Irene.” Take your finger and make the motion of ringing a doorbell right between her eyes, and say, “I ring, I ring, I ring.”

This is Jen. “Hi, Jen.” Put gemstones (for Jen) in the bags below her eyes.

This is Ken. “Hi, Ken.” See a can (for Ken) embedded in his forehead.

This is Tom. "Hi, Tom." See a tomcat clinging to both his ears.

This is Carolyn. "Hi, Carolyn." Visualize Christmas carolers (for Carolyn) singing Christmas carols on her lower lip.

Now let's see if you remembered all of their names using the Image Method.

This is ______________________________.

This is ____.

This is ____.

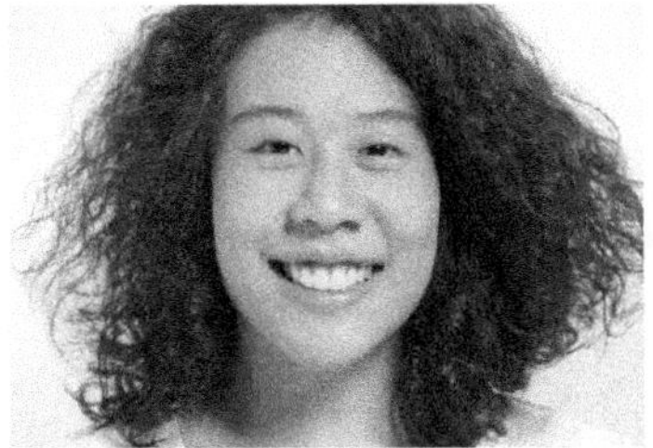

This is ____.

This is ______________________________________.

This is ______________________________________.

This is ______________________________________.

When I first learned this technique, I would practice by taking a magazine, giving all the faces a name, and then memorizing all the names using the Image Method. It worked for me, and it can work for you, too!

Now let's take remembering others one step farther.

Let's say a recent acquaintance Tom Burnside walks up to you. Imagine you've only met him once before. How powerful would it be not only to say, "Hi, Tom," but to say, "Hi, Tom, how's your wife Ann? How's your daughter Peggy's high school basketball coming along? Have you played golf lately in this beautiful weather?" Tom would be absolutely blown away by how great your memory is and by how considerate it was for you to remember all of that material. There would be an instant connection between the two of you, and Tom would probably try to reciprocate the same consideration toward you.

I have a memory technique that teaches you how to remember four or five things about someone in addition to their name. I share this technique in my online memory training, and I would like to share it with you. All you have to do is go to **bobkittell.com/names** and use this access code: **C7K-VCK8RX4**. This access code redeems you a chapter in my memory course, completely free!

***

Your mind is an amazing thing. It has the potential to remember the names of everyone you ever meet. Why does remembering someone's name matter to them? Because it does. It shows you care. People love hearing their names. There are a few exceptions: if you are in a police lineup or in the dentist's waiting room, you might not want to hear your name called out. But generally, when someone calls you by name, you feel acknowledged and respected.

Remembering the information of others creates connections with the people you encounter, the people who may play a significant role in your life once you make connections with them. And it all starts with remembering a person's name.

CHAPTER SEVEN

From Drinking Poison to Drawing Peace

"Revenge is like drinking poison and hoping the other person dies."

—Unknown

Even though I passed up the opportunity to take my memory program to television, my business was going great. My tour of over 150 college campuses was helping thousands of students, helping my business grow, and helping spread the word about the effectiveness of memory training. But then a major setback crept in.

My best friend from college betrayed me and destroyed my business. I watched something I had built vanish right before me. I watched as the business I had poured my heart into, the business I loved, the business that had brought me so much success, begin to profit the person who stole it from me. I had no choice but to let everyone go. I closed the door on a very lucrative business.

But this wasn't the end of it. No way. I had solid evidence that my friend had broken into my home and stolen my material, and I was prepared to press as many charges against him as I could. I'd get him back for what he had done. I turned the evidence over to the authorities, and they assured me his actions were criminal and they would bring him to justice. I was satisfied, knowing he would soon pay for what he had done.

My problem should have been solved then, right? But now I had a new problem: I was miserable. And the more I thought about what he had done to me, the angrier I got and the more miserable I felt. I couldn't sleep. I was angry, more than angry; I was filled with fury and frustration. There is no pain that matches the feeling of being betrayed by someone close to you. Every waking thought of mine was consumed with what he had done to me and what he deserved because of it. I had a constant knot in the pit of my stomach. I might not be able to restore my business, but I was going to get him back. I'd right this wrong.

I reached a point where it felt like I was dying inside, and I needed some help dealing with this situation, so I went to my old college professor for guidance. I told him what had happened. Every detail poured out of me like hot acid. The more I talked, the angrier I got. "Why am I suffering?" I asked him. "I didn't do anything wrong. My "friend" is the one who did wrong, so why am *I* so miserable?"

I went back and forth with my mentor on several matters about the situation and the way I was feeling about it, until finally he asked, "If you press charges, if you get this guy, if you really nail him, will that save your business?"

"No. The damage has been done," I replied angrily.

"Then why are you pressing charges if it won't make a difference?"

Frustration welled up inside me. "You've gotta be kidding! Someone has to teach him a lesson! Someone has to make it right! Someone has to teach him that he can't get away with this kind of thing!"

"Bob, that sounds like revenge. Revenge is like burning down the house to get the rat. Revenge is taking poison and hoping the other person dies." He told me that he understood my feelings and that I didn't have to listen to him or believe what he was telling me. He paused, then continued: "Bob, if you will let this thing go—look to the future, not to the past—I promise you, great new doors will open in your life." He let that soak in for a moment and then emphasized, "Bob, let this go before it destroys you."

It took a lot of thought, but eventually I told him I was willing to try. And I did. I tried it. I tried for two weeks to let it go. But I couldn't.

One day, while I was still desperately trying to figure out how to let this situation go, an arresting question came to me: *What is it you're thinking about?*

"Well, I'm thinking about how my best friend betrayed me, how he destroyed my business, how this isn't fair..."

Then another thought interrupted my mental tirade: *Can you think about some good things your friend has done for you before this situation occurred?*

I paused. There was that time in graduate school when I had run out of money and he handed me $1,500 cash and said, "Here's your graduation present in advance. This'll help you finish your degree." Another time, I had a foot operation during the holidays and he showed up at my door with a rented wheelchair to take me out to enjoy a Christmas Eve at the mall. More memories came back to me. My mind began to flood with great memories shared between my friend and me. I felt the anger and hatred, the depressing blackness, the "yuck," drain from my heart. They were replaced with intense gratitude for everything my friend had done with me and for me over the past eight years.

The next day, I called him and told him that I had dropped the charges. I then gifted him the business, gave him my blessing, and sincerely told him I wished him the best of luck. Can you imagine his reaction? He was sure something was up. Suspiciously, he replied, "Okay, Bob, what is it you really want?" I thought for a second and said from my heart, "What I really want is my friend back." When I hung up the phone, a giant weight had been lifted from my shoulders. The police, and many others who knew what had happened, thought I was an idiot for letting him go and letting him get away with what he had done. Were they right?

Two years later, he was killed in an automobile accident. When I got the news, all I could think was: *Aren't you glad you let it go?* A wave of understanding, appreciation, and gratitude washed over me. If I had pressed charges against my friend and ruined him, no change would have come to me, and I would have felt guilty for the rest of my life after his car wreck. But because I chose to let it go, I had set myself free from a lifetime of pain and regret.

I hope this story helps others who are holding onto grudges, whether it be toward a family member, friend, or even yourself. The only way to move forward in life is to first let go of the resentment. I know it's hard, but only good things come from letting go of resentment. Even in a situation like mine, where my business, everything I had built, was stolen from me, good things started happening once I let go of my anger and resentment. New doors were soon to open, and it was up to me to step through them, something I could never have done while lugging around anger and resentment.

***

The funny thing about opportunity is that you never know when it is going to pop up. After the incident with my friend stealing my memory training material, I was searching for my next move. I wasn't ready to give up on memory training just yet, but I needed a new approach to the matter.

I still use my memory techniques in just the basic, everyday routine of life. For instance, each morning when I wake up, I have visually placed reminders on my body to help me remember important things I need to know for that day. This system is called the Anatomy Method, and here's how it works: As you are preparing for the next day before you go to bed, think of all the tasks you have to do or things you want to accomplish. Now convert each task or thing into an image that will help you remember that item (similar to how we used the Image Method to remember someone's name). Next, you want to place each image on different parts of your body and visualize each image at that location. Then when you wake, move from location to location on your body, visualize what you placed there the night before, and remember everything about the day that is ahead of you!

So let's put this method into practice. Tomorrow I have to mow the lawn. I imagine grass growing on the top of my head and a tiny mower cutting it down. I also have to go to the bank. I imagine a dollar bill pinned to my forehead with a red thumbtack. On the way home from the bank, I need to pick up chicken from the store. I imagine a chicken perched on my shoulder, pecking at my ear. I also want to try and change a life. Diapers need to be changed. I imagine a dirty, stinky diaper in the palm of my hand. Now it's time for bed. I go to sleep with these images attached to my body. I wake up the next morning and move from head to toe visualizing the images I placed at each point the night before.

This is just one example of the way memory training had positively affected how I went through my everyday life, even after my memory business was stolen. But still, I was wondering what the next move was for me and memory training.

I ran into my friend Dave Craig, the first person I had shared my memory techniques with. He was working for a company that sold programs on speed-reading and memory skills. The company he worked for was expanding and needed another speaker to sell their memory program from the stage. Dave asked me if I was interested. Here was a door that had just popped out of nowhere, and I wasn't about to miss another opportunity, so I accepted Dave's offer.

This company sent me all over the country speaking to audiences of 500 or more. I discovered that I was really good at promoting courses and training from stage—and it was fun.

I would practice and practice . . . and practice. I got my entire presentation down, word for word, pause for pause. If I was allotted sixty minutes to speak, I would take it to the minute. To prepare, I would tell a story repeatedly to my friends, family, and co-speakers until I fleshed it out. Then I paid neighborhood kids twenty dollars each to listen to me practice my presentation live. I was ready.

I spoke at over 150 events that first year. It was an incredible experience. I became known in the industry as the hardest-working speaker the promoters had ever seen, and soon became the company's top memory speaker.

As I traveled about the country, I discovered some interesting phenomena. Different audiences in different parts of the country behaved differently. On the east coast, audiences generally arrived early. As you moved farther west, the audiences arrived later and later, until eventually, on the west coast, the audience might not reach capacity until forty minutes after the event began. If I was speaking in the southeast, people would be laughing out loud, practically rolling in the aisles. If I was speaking in the northeast, my presentation was often met with silence. Then someone would walk up afterward and comment, "That was great. You were funny."

I worked with this company for two years and loved every minute of it.

It had now been a few years since the first memory program had aired on television—the door I didn't step through. I began to wonder if I could, or should, put a recorded or printed program of my own together. Others thought it was a good idea and were willing to partner with me. I negotiated a joint venture with a company that produced infomercials. I agreed to put up fifty thousand dollars to produce the books, tapes, and an infomercial to test-market a memory program nationwide.

It was quite a moment, sitting outside the company's president's office with the papers drawn up and my fifty-thousand-dollar check in hand. This represented most of the money I had saved up from years of speaking. It was a significant risk. I considered changing my mind and walking away from the deal, but a strong feeling came over me that I shouldn't pass up another opportunity like I did the last time. So I went through with my fifty-thousand-dollar investment and produced my program. I had hundreds of videotapes produced in anticipation of a successful infomercial campaign...

And it failed miserably. The project was canceled, and I was left with a warehouse full of videotapes. But deciding to follow the opportunity of producing my program in video form led me to another open door.

A promoter started a series of live "success seminars." Brian Tracy, one of the most prolific sales trainers and speakers on the planet, was their lead-off speaker. They conducted three live events a week across the country with 1,500 or more in attendance at each event. It was big.

My business partner was speaking at these events, and I would occasionally attend just to watch him present. One day, Brian Tracy had a scheduling conflict and the promoter didn't have a keynote speaker for his seminar, so I told the promoter that I had an idea for kicking off the event. I would open with my keynote on memory skills and auction off my memory video to set the mood and warm up the audience. He was intrigued and willing to give it a shot.

During my presentation, I said, "I am holding my ninety-minute video program on memory training. This is the actual training I've given to tens of thousands of students at over 150 major universities across the United States. When your children watch this video they will smile, they will giggle, and, more importantly, they will memorize over one hundred bits of important information—terms, definitions, formulas, equations, names, and faces. The person in the room who wants it the most will get it. Here's how we'll make it fair: we'll do an auction. Everyone stand up. Who would like to have this video for yourself, your children, or the school your child attends for five dollars? Ten dollars? Fifteen? Twenty? Sit down when you're no longer interested in purchasing this video."

And, of course, a few sat down after just ten or fifteen dollars.

But then there were always people that were extremely interested and willing to pay a higher price for my memory video.

"Twenty-five? Thirty? Thirty-five? Forty?"

I usually stopped when there were about thirty people left standing; it was generally around the one-hundred-dollar mark. There were a few times, though, that the bid would go up as high as a thousand dollars, with some still willing to bid higher.

With the thirty people left standing, I would invite them to the front of the stage and address them: "Congratulations on putting such a high value on education. Ben Franklin said the best place to pour your money is into your head. I have a surprise for you. You can't have this video for a hundred dollars, but you can have it for twenty dollars. All in favor say aye."

After a resounding aye, I'd say, "I have one more surprise for you. You have my permission to make a copy of the videotape and donate it to a school of your choice, as long as you don't charge them for it. I can't be everywhere, but you can help me get this training into the schools. All in favor say aye."

I directed them to the tables around the room where they could get their videos, and while they dashed for the tables, I would say, "The rest of you are probably thinking, 'Gee, I wish I could have gotten the video for my kids and their school for twenty bucks.' Well, I'll tell you what, for the next two minutes, or as long they last, you can. Go, go, go! Get up out of your seats right now and get them while you can."

It was a great idea, it was a lot of fun, and it worked! When you figure that my audiences averaged 1,500 people and over half of them would purchase a video, well, that's a lot of memory videos—that's a lot of money! I sold the entire stockpile of videos I had in storage. It wasn't the way I had originally intended. No, that door had closed, but another had opened, a better door. For years, I sold thousands of videos to live audiences; first on VHS tapes, then on DVDs, and now they stream online—all because my fifty-thousand-dollar investment in a television infomercial had failed.

CHAPTER EIGHT

The Power of Pause

"I think 99 times and I find nothing. I stop thinking, swim in silence, and the truth comes to me."

—Albert Einstein

"Here is a five-dollar bill. I'm going to sell it for one dollar. Does that interest anyone?"

This scenario is one of my favorite bits to perform onstage. I pull out a five-dollar bill and ask that question, and I hold out my other hand to take someone's dollar.

"The offer is good for ten seconds; then the deal expires. Ten . . . nine . . ."

People in the audience are mumbling, digging into their pockets or purses, raising their hands.

"Eight . . . seven . . ."

Some hold up a dollar bill.

"Six . . . five . . . four . . ."

Finally, someone jumps up, runs to the stage, and puts a dollar in my hand with a split second left before the offer expired.

"Give him a round of applause! See—it's not hard to be successful. One person did something that thousands didn't even try to do. He took action!"

There are three kinds of people: those who wonder what happened, those who watch things happen, and those who make things happen.

"Now I have a twenty-dollar bill I'm going to sell for ten dollars. Ten . . . nine . . . eight . . ."

This time several people jump up and race toward the stage. The fastest one wins the prize!

"Okay, here's a hundred-dollar bill—but I'm not stupid." I always get a big laugh after this comment. "But remember, taking action is important. Taking action is how you get results. And, by the way, did you know that when you take action you have the power to change other people's lives?"

People are always caught off guard by this transition, like they realize my giving money away is over and I am back to being serious.

I continue: "Let me demonstrate. Who could use some cheering up? Now, be honest, who's had a tough day, maybe a tough week? Maybe you just received some bad news or have just had some misfortune lately."

Usually someone in the audience will point to a friend sitting next to them. I ask that person, "Could you use some cheering up? Well, your friend thinks so. Come on up here. Don't be nervous; there's only 20,000 people staring at you right now."

As this person comes onstage, I ask their name. "Hi, Kathie. My name is Bob, B-O-B. You can spell it the same way forward or backward. I bet you didn't think *this* was going to happen to you today."

I say to the audience, "Kathie could use some cheering up. Would you like to help me cheer her up? Great! This is what we're going to do: on the count of three, let's give Kathie a standing ovation. No, not a normal ovation, a *standing* ovation. An ovation meant to cheer her up. An ovation to knock her socks off. An ovation where people outside are wondering, who's the famous rock star onstage? Ready—one . . . two . . . three!"

The applause that follows is perhaps the most memorable and heartfelt moment of the entire event. Be it a high school auditorium of students, a company retreat, or an inspirational event with thousands in an arena, the audience rises as one and deafening applause erupts and, like a wave, support and positivity wash onto the stage.

As the applause fades, I turn to Kathie and say, “Could you feel that? Wasn’t that amazing? And, oh yeah, I have one more thing for you. Remember that hundred-dollar bill?” Her eyes get real big as I take it out of my pocket and hand it to her. “It’s yours.”

As she leaves the stage, I announce dramatically, “Kathie is feeling better! But not only is Kathie feeling better, who else is feeling better?” The audience responds with, “We are!” I then say, “Isn’t that amazing? You can’t *give* kindness away. It’s always returned. If you’re ever feeling down, depressed, or lonely, go do something for someone.”

***

There is something else every single person can do every single day to positively affect the people they come into contact with. It’s called the Power of Pause.

When somebody is talking to you, what are you doing? Are you actually hearing what they are saying? Or are you thinking about what you are going to say next? Are you thinking about how you could correct them? Teach them? Fix them? Are you passing judgment without actually hearing what they are saying? Perhaps you are thinking of a story that is better than the story they are telling and just can't wait for your turn to talk. Well, the fact is, when you are focused on what you are going to say next, you aren't really listening to what the other person is saying.

We've all been in a conversation where the person you are talking to jumps on top of what you are saying, and then you respond by jumping on top of what they are saying, and the pattern of interrupting each other takes over. That's not a conversation; that's a competition.

Try this while visiting with a bunch of friends: tell everyone your elbow hurts, and watch the competition begin, with everyone jumping in to tell you about their aches and pains. I realized this concept of conversations being competitions and began to think about how I could fix that issue. And then I decided to put my idea to the test.

Whenever I had a conversation with someone, I decided to listen and focus strictly on what they were saying. My teacher James Hadlock calls this aspect deep listening. I learned to be completely present, mentally and emotionally, while the other person was talking. It was simply listening, but listening at a deeper level.

After they had finished talking, I waited a few seconds before responding. This act is the Pause. During this pause, I reflected on what was said and commented in a way that moved the conversation forward.

The Power is the outcome. Often, the person had more to say and would continue to talk. But when they were actually finished speaking and I paused to reflect on what was said before commenting, the connection built was phenomenal. The people I was conversing with felt that I was respecting their opinions and thoughts, and gave me the same respect when I was speaking. The pace and direction of the conversation was completely different from how conversations usually are.

Now I can sit with the people I know and simply listen. In some cases, they'll talk for thirty or forty minutes. Afterward, they tell me they just divulged more information to me than they ever had to anyone else in their life. They can't believe the closeness or the level of connection. I've been told this many times by both friends and strangers.

A friend of mine had attention-deficit/hyperactivity disorder (ADHD). His mind raced constantly, and he couldn't sit still. I asked if he was open to trying a type of listening I had been practicing called Deep Listening and also the Power of Pause, and he said he was willing to give it a shot. Thirty minutes later, he was speaking slower and seemed very calm. His comment to me about Deep Listening and the Power of Pause was, "Dude, you're blowing my mind."

I have worked with former NFL football players filled with nervous energy and watched them calm down right before my eyes as I engaged them in Deep Listening and the Power of Pause.

I engaged a student in Deep Listening and the Power of Pause in an auditorium of 400 eighth-grade students. Not only was the connection felt between me and the student, but the entire audience was caught up in the connection.

These are just a few of the countless interactions I have had with individuals where the Power of Pause has had a positive impact on the connection built between people during a conversation.

It's a common phenomenon to have a fast-paced conversation filled with interruption, so don't worry if you find yourself in this situation. But when you do catch yourself in this situation, try to change the pace of the conversation by using the Power of Pause. Here's an example of how to do that:

When someone says, "Like a good neighbor . . . ," what is your impulsive response? I bet it's ". . . State Farm is there." That's my impulsive response too. But what if, instead of interrupting someone to finish that sentence, you paused for a moment to see what else emerges?

Perhaps you'll remember a neighbor who mowed your lawn when you were sick or injured, or watched your pets when you went out of town, and you comment about that memorable neighbor instead. Maybe the result is the person you are talking with offers to be a good neighbor to you if you ever need assistance, and then you offer to do the same for them. And already, a stronger connection is built between the two of you, just from using the Power of Pause once.

The Power of Pause extends to more than just conversations; it applies to our actions, too. Sometimes, it is best to pause and reflect on what we are about to do instead of acting impulsively. A simple pause can lead to a different, better response.

I learned how the Power of Pause impacts our actions one day when I was in the car with my daughter, Dolly, and she decided to unbuckle her car seat and maneuver out of it while I was driving. Isn't that a great day in the life of a parent?

I was heading down the freeway; I glanced into the rearview mirror and saw her out of her car seat. I authoritatively said, "Get back in your car seat, Dolly."

There was no response. I looked into the rearview mirror again and saw her looking back at me. Her arms were crossed defiantly, and she had a dismissive expression on her face that clearly said, "Yeah right."

I got a little irritated. "Get back in your car seat or else." And she continued to stare defiantly at me through the rearview mirror, as if to say, "Bring it on."

I pull the car over to the side of the freeway and got out, thinking, *I know how to solve this. I'm bigger than she is. I can wrestle her into her car seat.*

I got out of the car and began to walk around to open her door, but instead of acting on my first impulse, I paused. I looked heavenward and said out loud, "She's your daughter. What do you want me to do with her?"

And the response in my head was, "Give her a hug."

I paused again and said, "I'm not feeling like a hug. You got any more ideas?"

The reply was, "If you're not going to listen, don't ask anymore." So I decided to give it a try. I mean, nothing else had worked in the past.

I opened her door to find her standing there defiantly, ready for yet another fight. But instead of fighting with her, I put my arms out and calmly said, "Come give Daddy a hug."

Her defiant expression instantly softened and melted right before my eyes. She ran across the car, jumped into my arms, put her tiny little arms around my neck, and began to sob. Now, do you think a connection was made there?

When she was done crying, I asked if she was ready to go home, and she said yes. We didn't have another problem all the way home.

That is what I call the Power of Pause.

I told this story at a conference once, and a young lady asked me, "What do you do when someone is toxic and always seems to have something mean to say? She also happens to be family. I just don't know what to say to her when she acts that way. She drives me nuts!"

I responded with a metaphor: A man is walking through the woods and sees a lost dog. He reaches out to pet him, but the dog snarls and tries to bite him. The man's immediate reaction is that this is not a nice dog, and he yells, "Bad dog! I don't want anything to do with you. I'm not going to help you." The man turns on his heel and walks away.

Now take the same scenario with the man having an understanding of the Power of Pause. The dog snarls, tries to bite him, but instead of acting impulsively, the man pauses to observe and think about the situation. During this pause, he notices the dog's paw is caught in a muskrat trap, and his foot is lacerated and bleeding. The dog is reacting out of fear and pain. Now with a better understanding of the situation, the man helps the dog, and the dog's demeanor completely changes. He is no longer snarling, but instead is friendly and grateful to be out of the situation he was in.

When people lash out or are rude, it has nothing to do with you. It is always something else in their life that is causing them pain or negativity. I now see a person in pain.

I told the young lady who asked the question to apply this metaphor to her situation and see if it would work. What if, in the moment they lashed out at you, you paused and your reaction was to become intensely curious about what they were thinking and feeling? What if you just said, "Okay, talk to me," then just listened to whatever they had to say?

When you use the Power of Pause and wait to see and hear what is going on, eventually all their energy is exhausted. Watch for them to exhale. Notice their shoulders loosen and drop just a little. Often, in that moment, you will instinctually know where to go next with that person.

By not getting caught in a judgment about them, and instead remaining open to understanding, you put yourself in a position to help them through whatever is happening in their life. You put yourself in a position to build a stronger connection with someone who really needs it. I encourage everyone to try the Power of Pause when conversing with people or handling situations, and just feel what a difference it makes to the situation!

CHAPTER NINE

The Peace that Passes Perspective

"We are not endeavoring to get ahead of others, but to surpass ourselves."

—Hugh B. Brown

Since my public speaking and memory training career had been going so well, I was in a position to ask myself, *What do I want?* And I came to the conclusion that, career-wise, the most important thing was to decide for myself when to work and when to stay home and play with my kids.

Having worked at Provo Canyon Boys School for troubled youth as a counselor, I realized that many of the boys were there because their parents didn't have time for them. Whether their parents gave them everything or they had nothing wasn't as important as the fact that most boys there seemed to have been neglected. They had no real connection with their parents, no boundaries, and they were left to figure life out on their own.

That was not going to happen to my kids. I was determined to be available to my children no matter how busy I became. But speaking three days a week, fifty weeks out of the year wasn't allowing me to be at home enough for that to happen.

I partnered up with the best speaker I knew in the industry, Dave Craig. We both wanted the same thing: plenty of time to spend with our children so we could give them the best possible chance at a healthy childhood. We decided to tour as one speaker, taking turns as that speaker. I would go speak at events for three days, then take ten days off. Then Dave would speak at events for three days and take ten days off.

As we moved upward and onward in our career, we began to tour with some of the biggest names in the world. We shared the stage with celebrities in politics, entertainment, sports, and motivational or inspirational speaking. A whole gambit of personalities would be gathered backstage. Some were the most lovable, wonderful, down-to-earth folks you would ever know. Terry Bradshaw is one of the most authentic, talented speakers I've ever had the privilege of meeting. Barbara Bush, wife of former President George Bush, genuinely welcomed everyone with kindness and grandmotherly love. It was so refreshing to meet these people and realize their personalities were actually as genuine in real life as their celebrity personas seemed to be.

There were also some surprises, some not-so-genuine personalities. Imagine watching someone talking to thousands about health and nutrition and then seeing them later backstage eating a cheeseburger and greasy fries. Or watching someone talk brilliantly about the fundamental principles of success, yet battling depression and anxiety—and hiding it. Some came off as though they were the happiest, luckiest, kindest, most successful people on the planet, but offstage looked down on others as if they were not worthy of their time. Some of the speakers promoted principles that didn't really work, but they cashed in anyway.

I knew my memory training had already helped thousands, but I wanted to reach millions. So I continued to speak on memory training, one event at a time.

"How many of you just think about doing a little bit of studying and already you're tired? How many of you get to the third page of a book and can't remember what was on the first page? How would you like to spend less time studying and have more free time to do what you want to do?"

These lines are often the beginning of a presentation I give when speaking to college students. I follow this opening with a quick demonstration to show them how memory skills have worked for me.

"Let me show you how amazing these memory techniques are. I want you to randomly list twenty items by number as fast as you can on a piece of paper. For example, you might say number one is a camera, number two is a tree. As you write down each item, say it out loud. By the time you get done writing down all twenty items and saying them out loud once, I will have memorized the entire list without looking at the paper."

There are always some skeptics and those students who want to stump me. But after the twenty-item list is finished, I say, "Go ahead now and say any number and I will tell you the corresponding item that matches."

"What was number eight?" I respond with elephant. "What was number fourteen?" I say window. As I get each one of the numbers and corresponding items correct, their amazement builds.

"Would you believe me if I told you I only scored a 970 on my SAT?" Someone always laughs. "And that I struggled in college, living in the library usually fifty to sixty hours a week, only to get average grades? So how was someone like me able to train their brain to be as sharp as I have just demonstrated?"

With a simple technique called the Resemblance Peg System. I actually thought I was the creator of this system, but found out later it was actually created and used hundreds of years ago. The Resemblance Peg System is a mental filing technique that uses a series of pre-memorized concrete nouns that correspond with numbers. The title "peg system" refers to the fact that these concrete visual images allow us to "file" information in our mind for storage and retrieval. There are actually several different kinds of peg systems, and I go over the different kinds in my online memory training, but I'm going to focus on the Resemblance Peg System to show you how powerful this technique can be.

Think about what object each number looks like. Number one looks like a post, number two looks like a swan, and so on. On the next page, there is a list and chart of numbers one through twenty and what object each number corresponds to.

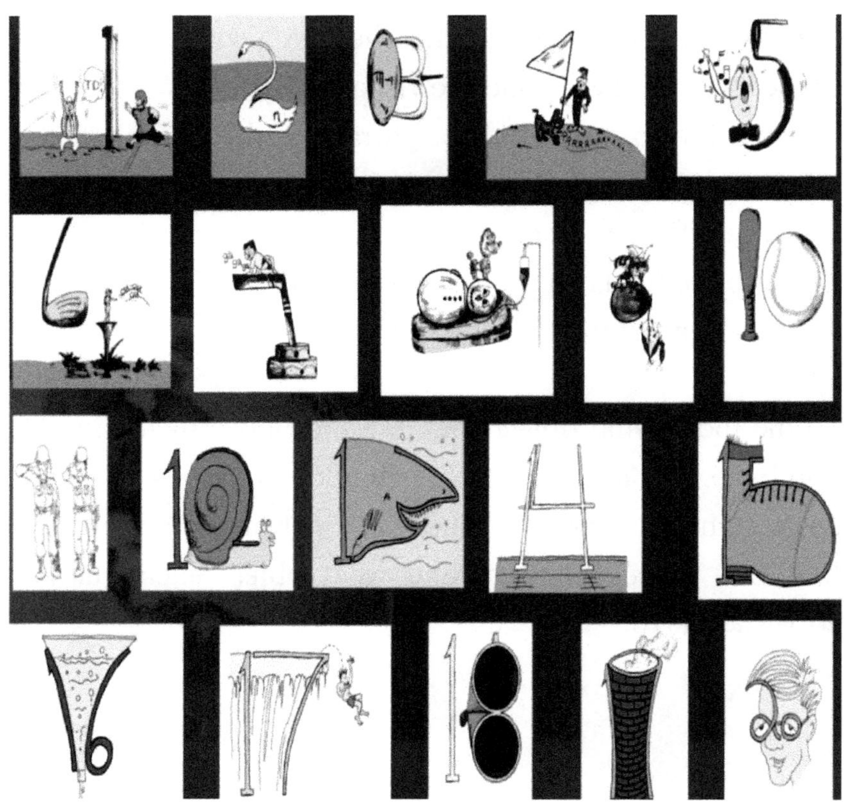

1. Post
2. Swan
3. Pitchfork
4. Flag
5. Sickle or hook
6. Golf club
7. Hockey stick
8. Snowman
9. Balloon
10. Ball and bat
11. Soldiers
12. Snail
13. Shark
14. Goal post
15. Boot
16. Funnel
17. Cliff
18. Shotgun

The first step is to study the chart and remember the corresponding image for each number. After that, you can remember orders, dates, lists, and much more!

ORDERS: Say you had to remember the order of the presidents of the United States. Washington was the first president, so visualize a post crossing the Delaware. Adams was the second president; visualize a swan in place of your Adam's apple.

DATES: If you had to remember the Russian Revolution was in 1917, visualize a Russian sitting on a smokestack (19) while falling off a cliff (17).

LISTS: Remember to, first, visit the dentist and, second, mail a letter today. Visualize a post in your dentist's hand and a swan swallowing your letter.

Here's how I use the Resemblance Peg System to rapidly remember the twenty items students name in an onstage demonstration. The student said number eight was an elephant and then wrote it on his paper. While he's writing it down, I visualize a snowman riding an elephant. He said fourteen was a window, so I visualize a window being thrown through a goal post like a football. Then, when I'm being quizzed and the student says, "What is number eight?" I visualize a snowman and the picture of him riding an elephant pops up. You should try this with your friends and family. You'll dazzle them!

If you recall, I told you in chapter one that the brain is a mental filing system and I have 150 inspirational quotes memorized by knowing how to operate this filing system. Well, now that you have learned the Resemblance Peg System, you can also learn how to memorize and file quotes away in your brain!

STEP 1: Identify the quote, saying, idea, principle, or poem you would like to memorize.

STEP 2: Read over the quote several times focusing on the imagery of the quote.

STEP 3: Identify a keyword or mental picture that captures the main idea of the quote.

STEP 4: Use the Resemblance Peg System to visually connect the keyword with a correlating number.

Here's how it looks in practice:

1. "A man who watches the clock generally remains one of the hands." —Unknown
2. "Anyone who is coasting along has to be going downhill." —Abraham Lincoln
3. "You can't just go on being a good egg. You must either hatch or go bad." —C. S. Lewis

The number one looks like a post, and a keyword for this quote could be a clock. So visualize a post jabbed through a clock. The number two looks like a swan, and the key image could be a wagon going downhill. Visualize a swan riding a wagon down a hill. The number three looks like a pitchfork, and a keyword for this quote could be an egg. Visualize a pitchfork stabbing a hard-boiled egg.

I use this system to file 150 quotes in my brain that I can recall anytime. When I'm onstage and ask someone to call out a number for me to state the corresponding quote, I visualize the resemblance of the number they call out, then I see the keyword or image connected to that number, and finally the quote flashes in my mind because of the keyword.

***

I'm not one of those people who stand onstage and advertise a program or product that I don't believe in. But there was a time when I felt like I was a different person onstage than I was offstage.

Onstage, I was confident, enthusiastic, and inspirational, but offstage I was a mess. I had my dream job, only worked when I wanted to, and was making more money than I ever thought possible. But for some reason I started experiencing panic attacks.

In 2011, an event in my life flipped some kind of switch

in my brain. I awoke one morning drowning in a massive panic attack. I couldn't think. It was more than horrible. I had no idea what was going on. From that day forward, I'd experience two or three of these, sometimes more, in the course of a day.

I'm sad.
I'm never happy.
I'm frustrated.
I can't think.
I want to scream.
I have a deep, aching pit in my stomach.
My throat is tight . . . choking . . . can't breathe . . . My chest is going to burst.
My feet feel like they are on fire.
My head is about to explode.
This pain is unbearable.
I can't go on another day.
What is happening to me?

They tell you to keep a journal of your experiences so you can look back and remember all the nice things you've experienced over the wonderful life your creator blessed you with, a life filled with wonder and challenges and successes. Well, my journal looked more like a journey into the depths of Hell. My escape, my refuge from the pain, was either playing golf or speaking onstage.

There in the Georgia Dome, in front of 30,000 people, or in

the Staples Arena in L.A. or the United Center in Chicago, I found relief. The moment I stepped onstage, the anxiety and panic completely disappeared. My head cleared and I felt great. Who would imagine being onstage in in front of 30,000 people would be a place of calm? But for me it was. Then I'd step off the stage, walk to the green room, and collapse into a fetal position, curled up on the floor, as waves of panic and suffering washed over me. I wanted to die.

When you panic, your brain switches into the fight-or-flight (or freeze) mode. Blood leaves your core (thus, the pit in the stomach) and your frontal lobe (hence, the hazy thinking), and rushes to your extremities (hence, the burning sensation in my feet). My entire day was spent in panic or anxiety—I'm talking *high* anxiety—often an unnamed, unreasonable, apparently without-cause panic. I suffered arrhythmia. I was a mess. This unnamed panic was destroying my health, my relationships, and my career.

At the pinnacle of my career, with more success than I had ever dreamed of, I was miserable. I played golf—a lot—and I spoke—a lot—because I didn't know how else to stop the panic. I had no idea what was wrong with me or how to fix whatever was happening to my mind and body. I spent thousands of dollars going to multiple counselors, psychiatrists, mental health professionals, and practitioners. No one had the answer. I was sinking into a deeper, darker, ugly hole. Along with my combined panic and anxiety came anger. During my darkest time, which went on for months,

I'd find myself looking at the clock each afternoon around 3:00 p.m. and wondering how I would make it to 4:00 p.m. I finally understood why people end their lives. It's not to end their lives. It's to end their pain. Eckhart Tolle said, "If there's something you don't like, do something. Change it, leave it, or accept it. All else is madness." I wasn't willing to accept what was happening to me, I couldn't leave it, so I was trying to change it. But it wasn't working. The search for help continued.

My medical doctor became extremely concerned. After four months, he said, "We have to figure this out. Your body can't take this kind of stress much longer and will soon start shutting down. You could die."

I learned when your body senses stress, a hormone releases that constricts blood vessels and contracts heart muscles. If you remain in this state, blood vessels begin to deteriorate, the heart constricts, and the intestines and immune system start shutting down.

My physician referred me to a psychiatrist, Ludmil Manov. After an in-depth evaluation, he informed me that my problem was not chemical, and he thought he could help me. Yeah right. I'd heard those words so many times I had stopped believing anyone could help me. Besides, this guy made me uncomfortable. I met with three more counselors and liked each of them. They were all certain they could help me. Each of them equally got me nowhere, and I became desperate.

I'm not sure where the idea came from originally, but somewhere on this difficult and extremely uncomfortable path, I learned that I should turn and face, as best I could, the source of my pain and move toward it until the pain faded and disappeared.

I returned to the psychiatrist in whose office I felt so uncomfortable. I was curious to see what he might do differently. All the psychiatrists that I seemed to like couldn't help. Maybe the one guy I *didn't* like could.

***

"You just broke eye contact. Why did you look away?"

"Whataya mean?" I snapped back. "Everybody looks up. What are you talking about? Don't you know about looking up? I have to look up to get the answer."

"Are you angry with me?"

"No! I'm fine!"

I wasn't fine; I was irritated and angry. But as soon as he asked that question, I *became* fine. I insisted I was fine. I pushed down the anger. *Hmm . . . maybe not such a good thing to do*, but I didn't know this yet.

I continued to look into his eyes while he asked a question

and then look away as I searched for an answer. Each time I looked away, he'd catch me at it and challenge me.

"Look at me. Don't break eye contact."

Each time he said that, my irritation increased. And then he would ask, "Are you angry with me?"

"No, I'm not angry," I would always say as I sat back and made myself not be angry.

Twice a week, I would see this psychiatrist, and nothing was happening—except he'd challenge me and I'd drop into denial. I wasn't making progress. The panic was out of hand; the depression was deepening.

Then finally one day, I decided to confront him head on. Driving to his office, I thought, *Maybe he wants me to be angry. Okay, I'll be angry.*

I went into his office, sat down, and before he could say a word, I leaned forward in my chair and confronted him: "Okay, if you want me to be mad, I'll be mad."

"Ah . . . so it looks like you're ready to go to work."

"Fine!"

"Okay. Are you angry with me?"

"Yeah, I'm angry with you!"

"Why?"

"Because I'm wasting hundreds of dollars, and we're getting nowhere!"

"Do you want to hit me?"

"Honestly? Yeah, I'd like to smack you."

He was sitting across the room and told me to physically take a swing and imagine hitting him. So I swung hard into the space between us.

He said, "So what happened?"

"I just decked you. Now I feel better."

"Look into my eyes. Now who do you see?"

I thought, *This guy is losing it!* I was tired of getting nowhere, but I looked into his eyes anyway. All of a sudden, I saw images of my earlier life: people I didn't want to face, things I had pushed away, feelings I had avoided.

This was my first big breakthrough. I was finally seeing for the first time how my life had become obsessive. How I was always trying to prove something. How I never felt good enough. As the sessions continued, the breakthroughs continued. I learned more about myself than I ever thought possible. I dug it all up and faced it. It was painful, but worth it.

***

The panic attacks and anger were vanishing. That was great. However, I still had to deal with four hours of high anxiety every morning. That was not so great. The search continued.

I discovered the power of positive thinking. I loved it. I embraced it. It changed my life. I went from having mostly negative thoughts to having mostly positive thoughts. And it really did help. Life got better. I began waking up each day as a *positive* anxious person.

Then I learned about the power of gratitude. I learned how gratitude helps us feel better. I studied gratitude. I mastered gratitude. I even spoke on gratitude. It was great. Life improved some more. I woke up each day as a very *grateful, positive* anxious person.

Then I learned about the power of happiness. I learned about smiles, laughter, power poses, things we can do to be happy. I got really good at it. I added happy exercises to my ever-growing check list of things to do each morning to feel good and make others feel good. Life improved again. I then woke up each day as a very *happy, grateful, positive* anxious person.

I then learned about the power of service. Wow! It was so simple! Yes! If I just serve enough people, I'll feel better. It was great. I started to be more service-oriented. Life got even better! I served all kinds of people in all kinds of ways. I then woke up each day as a *service-oriented, happy, grateful, positive* anxious person.

I learned about the power of meditation, yoga, affirmations, motivation, tapping, energy work . . . Every time I turned around I was adding a new remedy to my "box of bandages." I spent three hours every morning going through my service-oriented, happiness-focused, grateful- and positive-thinking checklist to battle anxiety.

There came a point where I had to admit it wasn't working so well. Enter James Hadlock.

Somewhere along the grapevine, James had heard he should meet with me, and I heard I should meet with him. When we finally met up with each other over lunch, I noticed that he and his wife had this calming aura about them that is hard to explain. James went on to tell me about the struggles and addictions he used to experience, and that he had overdosed more than sixty times in his life. I learned later that this is what showing one's authentic self was all about.

I proudly showed him my planner with this amazing checklist of things I did every morning to feel better, meaning not anxious.

He looked at it, then back at me, and said, "Bob. Do me a favor. Never look at that list again."

"What? You gotta be kidding me! Do you know how long it took me to put that list together?"

Then he asked me a very probing and profound question: "How's that been working for you?"

"Um . . . not so good."

"Bob, when something doesn't feel right, when we're experiencing something uncomfortable inside, we try to stay busy so we don't have to deal with it. Have you been doing that?"

"Um . . . well . . . yeah."

"I bet that hasn't helped your anxiety, Bob." It wasn't a question. He knew it. I knew it. I was addicted to busy. He continued, "The next thing we do is try to think differently about it."

"What do you mean?"

"You shifted from a negative to a positive; you changed ungrateful to grateful. That hasn't been working for you either, has it?"

That *was* a question. My answer was a simple and rather defeated no.

He went on, "Many try serving others to feel better. You tried that, right?"

"Yes, I did."

"That didn't work either, did it?"

"No." I was frustrated. "So . . . what do *you* got?"

"I'm going to show you how to get connected. Connect with others, connect with yourself, and everything will work itself out."

"Great! How you gonna do that?" I retorted.

He leaned back smiling. "I could put you in the trunk of my car, drive you up to a beautiful place like Park City (a beautiful resort town in the Wasatch Mountains), and you would get out, look around, and feel better. But the next morning when you woke up and found yourself right back where you started, with no idea how to get to Park City on your own, you'd be . . . well . . . right back where you started. I'm going to show you how to get there on your own."

It's like the old adage: Give a man a fish and you feed him for a day. Teach a man to fish and you feed him for a lifetime.

James took me over to the pool in the hotel where we were meeting. "If I hired you to keep that water calm, smooth, like glass and gave you an unlimited budget to accomplish that, what would you do?"

"I'd probably exceed the budget."

He laughed. "What *would* you do, Bob?"

"I would build walls around it, put a roof over it, put up a 'do not disturb' sign. That should keep it calm."

"Would that keep an earthquake from disturbing the water?"

"Well . . . no."

"Bob, is there really anything you can do to keep the water calm? When a storm blows in, even a little breeze, the water is disturbed, right? And if the storm is violent, the water is violently disturbed, right? Then what happens? What *always* happens to the water after a storm?"

The light went on. "Ah, yes. It gets calm again."

"You got it. When you have anxiety or anger or a more violent emotional storm, what do you do? You try to fix it. When you are upset, you try to *make yourself* calm down. You try to make *everything* calm down. You try to control it. You try to control you. It doesn't work."

He was right. It's like jumping into the pool and trying to

slap down all the waves and ripples. All we do is create an even bigger disturbance. This was another wonderful paradigm shift: understanding the flaw in my lifetime habit of fixing things that I couldn't fix or forcing solutions that shouldn't be forced.

But wait. There were things I really needed to deal with, so I pushed back a bit.

"James, what am I gonna do about my relationships and my job? There are so many directions I could go with my speaking. There are things about life . . ."

James said, "Imagine you drop a quarter into the shallow end of the pool. Now let's churn up the water. If you try and reach down and pick up the quarter, what happens? You'll miss it because of the distortion created by the agitated water. You have to wait until the water calms down before you can even know where the coin is, before you can even reach for it."

Another way to look at it is to imagine a snow globe. Shake it up. The snowflakes are swirling; it's like a storm in there. Can you see clearly in that globe? No. What do you have to do to see clearly? Wait for it to settle. The snowflakes are like your thoughts: when they're swirling around you can't think clearly. That's not the time to make decisions.

He continued, "Bob, you're confused as to what to do about

relationships, career, beliefs, and life in general. That's okay. It's a common thing. But you're trying to solve the problem with an agitated mind. Wait. Just wait. Let it calm. Like water, it always will. When it settles down and clears, you'll know what to do."

Eight months later, I realized how right he was. My relationships had improved, my career took off again, and I had a greater, deeper, better understanding of how the mind works, especially when you let it settle down and do its job.

When your brain has an event that triggers panic or anxiety, it needs to run its course—it *will* run its course—just like a storm at sea. The neurotransmitters have already fired off, releasing chemicals into your system that result in disturbance. This disturbance is called stress.

How do you calm it? What do you do? Well, nothing. Doing nothing is often the hardest thing to learn how to do. If something is wrong, we tend to try relentlessly to fix it, but if you focus on fixing the problem, you're focused on the problem. If you do nothing and let the disturbance calm itself, you are letting go.

***

After months of working on the root of my anxiety and pain, something amazing happened. I no longer had to play golf from sunup to sundown. On flights to speaking engagements, I could sit quietly on the plane looking out the window instead of forcing my mind to be occupied by simultaneously listening to a book and playing games on my phone. By treating the root instead of always putting a bandage over the symptoms, things finally started to change.

My mindset shifted from being overly intense and driven to being calm and peaceful. I began to see the world through more accepting eyes. And people were noticing.

One day, my son asked me what was going on. "Dad, you've never been able to sit still and just talk to me. You were like a mosquito on cocaine. It was fun as a kid because you were always go, go, go, from one activity to another. But now, Dad, it's so different. Just now you sat still for an hour and talked with me."

Friends started joking with me about what they called the "before" and the "after" Bob. "Who are you? What have you done with Bob?" I didn't know. I was asking myself the same question.

Shortly after my change, I jumped into a cab with another speaker I had known for over fifteen years. I told the cab driver the name of the hotel, and he hit the gas as if we were at the Indianapolis Motor Speedway. I leaned forward and calmly said, "Sir, I was in a rollover accident a year ago. I would appreciate it if you went slower."

The driver slammed on the brakes and slapped the steering wheel with both palms in frustration. He brought his car to a dead stop in the middle of the road, twisted in his seat, and glared at me as he snapped, "It's been a year. You should be over it by now!"

Only months earlier, that would have triggered a brutal response from me. Instead, I paused for a moment, reflected on what he had said, then replied calmly, "You're right, I should be over it, but my nerves are shot. I would appreciate it if you went slower."

The driver looked at me for a moment and, apparently reflecting my mood, replied calmly, "Okay."

As he drove off again, slower and more carefully this time, I thought he might be irritated, but surprisingly, he became friendlier. It was as if the incident and the ensuing interaction had transformed him from cabbie to tour guide, as he enthusiastically told us about all the sights we should see before we left Alaska.

After we exited the cab and entered the hotel, my friend turned to me and said, "What's happened to you? Five years ago you would have blown up and gotten angry with that cab driver." I explained to him how I had faced my anger head on and had eliminated it from the root. My mindset was completely different now.

Every year, I go to Sacramento to speak, and while I'm there, I always go to dinner with an old college friend and his wife. This time, after visiting for about an hour and a half, my friend turned to his wife and asked, "What's different about Bob?"

His wife responded to me instead of to him. She told me that she had never looked forward to dinner with me before because I made her a nervous wreck. "Bob, you couldn't sit still. You couldn't relax even for a minute, so I couldn't either."

My children and friends told me they liked the new Bob a lot better than the intense, driven, neurotic, fidgety Bob. My health improved. My arrhythmia vanished. The constriction in my throat vanished. The outbursts of frustration vanished. Daily massages to relieve tension in my upper back and neck were no longer needed.

I had no idea that suppressed memories could do so much damage.

CHAPTER TEN

The "Movies of the Mind" Monster

"Guilt is I made a mistake. Shame is I am a mistake."

—Brene Brown

You know, I have to admit that I've been talking up how boosting your memory can improve your life, but sometimes forgetting a memory is even more important. I read somewhere that if we have an emotional reaction that seems out of proportion with an event, it's likely rooted in a childhood trauma. That was certainly the case with me.

Whenever I saw a baby bird that had fallen out of its nest, my world would come to a standstill. I had to take it home and raise it. The first time I did this, the bird died. I went to the library to figure out why and found out little birds, such as sparrows and starlings, have to be fed every thirty minutes or they die, but that information didn't stop me from raising baby birds. I would sneak baby birds into school and feed them every thirty minutes, then sneak them back home and continue feeding them. From sunup to sundown, I stopped what I was doing every thirty minutes to make sure they got fed. Neighbors would call and tell me about a fledgling that had fallen out of its nest. I'd drop everything and go pick it up, bring it home, and take care of it. As an adult, I spent hundreds of dollars paying kids to take care of the birds when I was out of town. One summer, I had over twenty-five baby birds in my backyard. I was out of control.

One day, my daughter asked me why I stopped taking care of baby birds.

During one of my therapy sessions, a memory of me as a five-year-old came up. I had found a baby robin and tried to teach it how to fly. After repeated attempts of tossing the fledgling up and watching it fall to the ground, I became angry that it wasn't even trying to fly. In frustration, I slammed it into the ground, ending its already short life. My five-year-old self couldn't face the guilt and pain of that moment, and I buried the memory deep into my mind and refused to face my feelings about it.

It's my understanding that when you have a traumatic experience and attach an emotion to it, you create a neural pathway. Even though it was buried deep inside my mind, the memory of my reaction and the resulting death of the innocent bird created a strong neural pathway that was governing my behavior. Years later, as an adult, I was unconsciously trying to fix what I had broken. I had never faced the emotion until the memory flooded back in this therapy session. I wept. The pain dissipated and the grief subsided. The obsession left with the grief. I never again felt compelled to seek out and care for baby birds. The key was realizing what shameful memories were controlling my thoughts and actions.

I faced several shameful memories throughout my therapy sessions. I was healing, memory by memory; letting those stored emotions surface and then letting them go. Facing my shameful memories head on was how I was able to recognize my buried rage.

I've always been competitive—ridiculously competitive. Friends and clients have watched, dumbfounded, as I broke golf clubs against the ground or a tree (all the clubs in my bag have been victims of my rage), smashed racquetball rackets, and threw ping-pong paddles against the wall. I hated to lose. Fortunately, I attacked things, not people. Even when I felt rage toward someone for something they did or said, I never attacked them physically, but I had a tendency to attack them verbally. I have unloaded on promoters, getting right in their faces, not caring what the consequences might be. Luckily, my dear friend and partner usually patched things up after I ruffled their feathers. Actually, it was more like after I tore the feathers right off.

While I was going through therapy, something happened that brought my issue of rage to the forefront, thanks to my ever-observant counselor (by this time I liked him).

I was playing basketball when a competitor roughly hip-checked me and sent me flying. I managed to keep hold of the ball, which I promptly threw hard at his head, then charged him like an angry bull. This was not a particularly good idea, especially since he was much larger and stronger than me (rage does indeed deplete the frontal lobe, the thinking part of the brain, of blood and oxygen, and therefore, rationale). The other players restrained me until I calmed down.

Facing this memory in my therapy session, it occurred to me that my anger had nothing to do with the other guy. It had something to do with my past. Could it be that the person who's upset is the one with the problem? Many people try to blame another for how they feel. They claim that someone made them angry or upset. I learned it was my responsibility for what I think, feel, and do. If the rage is healed, no one can trigger it.

My counselor had me replay the experience in my mind. I imagined looking into the other players' eyes. As I did that, I saw the face of a coach who had treated me and my teammates like dirt. I allowed the rage to come up and sat with it, watched it, observed it, just felt it without judging it. Here's what I saw:

> *After losing 52–14, we arrived to practice the next Monday to find a piece of white athletic tape on each of our helmets. Written in black marker on each helmet was "I'm a loser." The marker was a permanent marker. The insult felt permanent as well. He did that to every one of us. Can you imagine an entire team going out to practice with "I'm a loser" on their helmets? Several players quit—good players including the starting quarterback.*

I continued to let the rage surface. I saw myself as a six-year-old, angry with my parents, then as a four-year-old, mad at God. I felt the pent-up emotions, anger, and frustration that had been fighting to get to the surface, like a drowning person fighting for air. Finally I let them surface. I let them breathe. I let them be seen, heard, felt, and experienced. And then I released them.

Michael Singer explains dealing with stored emotions best. In a lecture to students at a mindfulness conference at Miami University, he said, "It hurt when you pushed it down there. It's going to hurt when it comes out." I found this statement to be very true as I was facing my memories in therapy, but once they were released, I never had to feel that pain again.

My intense competitive nature changed. I stopped apologizing and feeling bad every time I missed a shot playing basketball or golf. I now play for the experience, not the score. In fact, I can play golf and not even keep score. It no longer bothers me to lose a game or make a bad shot. I stopped telling myself that I wasn't good enough. I stopped beating myself up for making a mistake, no matter how big of a mistake it was.

I had healed yet another part of my mind.

***

What if I told you that, throughout your day, your mind creates scenarios, or little stories, that take up way too much of your time and cause unnecessary anxiety? "Ninety-nine percent of our thoughts are a total waste of time, and they do nothing but freak us out."—Michael Neill. James helped me realize this aspect, and I was blown away that I had never realized it before. He told me, "When you find yourself in a 'story' based on the past or a prediction of the future, ask yourself, 'Without this story, what could I experience right now?'"

The biggest story playing in my head at the time was about a relationship with someone very important to me. There was the possibility that she might give our relationship another chance, and the different possible outcomes were creating extreme anxiety. There were two stories playing simultaneously in my head, over and over again, doubling my anxiety.

Story #1 ~ She *would* give me another chance.

That terrified me.

Story #2 ~ She *would not* give me another chance.

That terrified me.

My response to James was, "Without these stories I would be excited, contributing, and be a beam of light. But because of these stories, I'm getting my butt kicked today. My mind is going back and forth from high anxiety to massive depression."

He didn't respond right away, so I let the question percolate. *What would I experience without that story?* Then it hit me: I'd be at peace. Wow, what a way to live: at peace. Without this story, I'd be at *peace.*

I began to view these stories as "movies of the mind." When I'm watching a scary movie and feel deep-seated fear overtaking me, I remind myself that I'm watching a movie with actors and actresses and it's not real. I began to apply the same reminder to these scenarios that played in my head.

The idea of eliminating "movies" that play in your mind really sank in when a young friend of mine told me she was starting middle school the following week and she was scared.

I asked her, "Have you started school next week yet?"

"No," she giggled.

"Have you been given too much homework yet?"

She laughed again. "No."

"So the only place that movie is playing is in your head, right? And it isn't real, is it? If you keep replaying this movie, which hasn't happened yet, how does that make you feel?"

"Worried. Scared."

"Ahhh...so what would it feel like right now without that movie of your mind playing, the movie that isn't real?"

She got a big smile on her face and looked at her dad. "I'd be happy!"

In a similar situation, I helped another young girl understand that her anxiety was because she was allowing her mind to play "movies." I was having dinner with a friend and his family, and his daughter told me that she was getting really nervous about her next soccer game.

I asked, "When is your game?"

"This coming Saturday."

"What are you afraid of?"

"I'm afraid of falling down and the coach getting mad and yelling at me in front of everybody."

"What else are you afraid of?"

"That he'll take me out of the game."

"Today is Tuesday. Has next Saturday's game started yet?"

She looked at me like I'd lost my mind.
I pressed on: "Have you fallen down already in that game that hasn't started yet?"

"No."

"Is the coach yelling at you right now, here in the dining room?"

"No," she chuckled.

"Have you been taken out of the game yet, the one that isn't being played until this Saturday? Remember, today is Tuesday. What would it feel like right now without that movie playing in your mind?"

She sat with that for a moment; then her face lit up. "I'd be just fine." She started laughing. "You're blowing my mind!"

I explained that every time we feel anxiety about the future or sadness about the past, it's coming from a movie that isn't real.

A short time later, this same young lady started getting angry, and I asked her why. She started telling me about her sister and how mad she was about something she had said a couple days ago. Then she stopped and said out loud, "Wait, that was two days ago. It's over. It's just a movie, and the movie isn't real!" I watched a transformation occur right before my eyes as she became so excited about discovering this insight she had never seen before.

The problem with creating "movies" in your mind is that they seem and feel real. But think of it this way: if you're caught up in a scary movie, the emotions of fear, anxiety, etcetera, are real, but the projected images that are causing them are fake. It's Hollywood! The images aren't real. Your thoughts are projections playing in the theater of your mind. They are memories of the past or predictions of possible futures.

When you allow your mind to create fake "movies," the result is real, usually painful or anxious, emotions based on false images. Think about how many times you have worried about something that didn't happen. Get your mind under control, and stop letting these "stories" take up so much of your time. Once you're aware that the movies are not real, they will lose their power and stop taking up so much of your time.

CHAPTER ELEVEN

The Beauty of Building Better Bonds

"The dullest pencil is better than the sharpest memory."

—Mark Twain

(But if you don't have a pencil, this should work.)

One of my favorite memory skills to teach to live audiences is a method called the Loci System. *Loci* is plural for the Latin word *locus*, which means "place." The English word *location* comes from this term. This system is actually one of the oldest memory methods known. It was developed around 500 BC by a man named Simonides.

According to legend, Simonides was giving a speech at a great hall one evening. A messenger came and told him that a visitor awaited him outside. When Simonides went outside to see what the man wanted, the roof of the building collapsed, killing everyone inside.

The bodies of those inside were crushed beyond recognition. Simonides was the only one able to identify the victims, because he remembered the locations of the people around the table. This experience led him to reflect on a possible tool for memorization. He developed a principle based on linking items to be learned with certain physical locations (loci). The only limitation to this system was possessing knowledge of the locations used. The idea caught on and was used by Greek and Roman orators to help them memorize long speeches. It is possible that this is where the phrase "in the first place" originated.

There are only two steps to master the Loci System.

STEP 1:
Become personally familiar with a series of locations that are in a natural or logical sequence. These locations will serve as memory anchors for you. By keeping them in mind, you will never drift off into a sea of forgetfulness.

STEP 2:
Associate a mental image (the key here is clear visualization) of each item you are to remember with a particular spot. The pattern in which you arrange your locations depends upon the order you come to them in a mental stroll through the spots you have chosen to employ as anchors. One of the main advantages to this system is the concrete mental image you hold of locations since you are so familiar with them.

Let's put the Loci System in practice:

STEP 1:
Begin with a familiar location: your home. Obviously, homes vary, but I'll use some typical spots in this example to illustrate the point.

You walk up to the home and see the DRIVEWAY; we can call this area one. Area two will be the GARAGE, three the FRONT STEPS, four the KITCHEN, five the LIVING ROOM, six the BEDROOM, seven the BATHROOM, eight the ATTIC, nine the ROOF, and ten is the CHIMNEY.

STEP 2:
Now here's the scenario: A family member is giving you a list over the phone of items they need you to pick up at the store, and you do not have pencil and paper to make a shopping list. The Loci System will aid you in the completion of your shopping duties.

HAIRSPRAY is the first item on your list. Picture a giant can of hairspray on your DRIVEWAY.

Now go to area two, the GARAGE, and attach the second thing on your list, which is salt. Picture thousands of salt shakers stacked in your garage.

Next, imagine SPAGHETTI on your STAIRS.

Next, picture DOG FOOD covering your KITCHEN FLOOR.

Item number five is CELERY. Picture it growing in your LIVING ROOM.

CABBAGE all over your BEDROOM. What color is it, green or red? Is it shredded or a head of cabbage? Don't forget to be specific in your details!

This is followed by BREAD floating in the BATHTUB.

Now visualize POTATO CHIPS insulating the ATTIC.

Next, PORK CHOPS covering the ROOF like shingles.

And finally, LOBSTER sticking out of your CHIMNEY.

Now it's time to go shopping! Can you remember the logical order of items based on a mental walk-through of the house? Let's find out!

What was connected to the:

DRIVEWAY?
GARAGE?
STAIRS?
KITCHEN?
LIVING ROOM?
BEDROOM?
BATHROOM?

ATTIC?
ROOF?
CHIMNEY?

Now check your list for accuracy. Remember, this will get easier when you put it into practice using your own home or a place that you are personally familiar with.

Now that you have the basis down for the Loci System, let's discover how to expand the number of locations in an area, in case you have a larger number of items to remember. It's not as difficult as you think. Just expand the number of points in your house by being more detailed in your mental walk-through of the location. For example, near the driveway there is a mail box. In the garage, there is a toolbox. In fact, if you think for a moment, you can probably identify ten points in the driveway, ten points in the garage, and ten points in every room. By following a pattern of development like this, you can easily increase your location points from ten to one hundred and thus increase your loci memory capacity.

Here's an example of how to expand the number of locations in your home:

In your kitchen, you have:

- Cupboard
- Plates
- Glasses

- Bowls
- Pots
- Pans
- Utensils
- Fork
- Spoon
- Knife
- Sink
- Hot water
- Cold water
- Sprayer
- Drain
- Oven
- Stove
- Fridge
- Milk
- Butter
- Eggs
- Mustard
- Cheese
- Table
- Chairs
- Counter

In your bedroom, you have:

- Door
- Knob
- Rug

- Dresser
- Bed
- Nightstand
- Lamp
- Closet
- Shirt
- Pants
- Suit
- Ties
- Dresses
- Hangers

Instead of using your home time and time again, which increases the possibility of interference (i.e., having more than one bit of information in the same place), try using other loci. Hundreds of loci are at your disposal. Virtually anything that is concrete in your mind is fair game for loci.

Here are some examples of loci you could use:

- Current home
- House lived in during childhood
- Apartment lived in during college
- Grandma's house
- Aunt's house
- Best friend's house
- Elementary school
- High school
- College

- Cafeteria
- Restaurants
- Office

Any place that you are familiar with can serve as a loci to use as a memory tool! All you have to do is be able to mentally walk through that loci.

The Loci System is useful for more than just remembering lists.

A demonstration I currently use onstage at speaking events involves the audience remembering the original colonies of the United States in sequence using the Loci System. I just use locations around whatever room we are in.

"The first state is Delaware. Everyone look at that door where we walked in. If I say deli, what's the first image that comes to mind? Okay, deli sandwich. Everyone visualize sandwiches all over the door. Start chewing on the door for lunch."

"Above the door is an exit sign. That's where we will remember Pennsylvania. Pennsylvania reminds me of pencil. Everyone pick up a pencil and visually throw it at the exit sign."

"Visualize a giant New Jersey (a new sports jersey) hanging on the wall."

"Visualize Georgia peaches falling from the ceiling."

Continuing around the room, we place visual cues to remember the colonies. Then I have the entire audience repeat the sequence by doing a walk-through of the room. Everyone is amazed at their newfound skill. And it only took them a minute to learn!

***

Up to this point in my career, I had been to numerous colleges promoting my memory training; I had spoken at many different kinds of events; my memory training was on video, DVD, and online; I had a whole bag full of speaking demonstrations to perform onstage, but yet another opportunity came knocking on my door.

I was asked to speak to 400 eighth-graders about bullying and consequences. This event was my first time speaking strictly to a group of teenagers. I wasn't sure what to expect, but I decided to give it a whirl anyway.

I used some of the same speaking techniques that I used at business conferences and other events, like a few jokes and inspiring stories from my past. I was truly surprised to find I had the students' complete attention. It was amazing! Even more amazing was that, each year, I was invited back to speak to the next class of eighth graders.

I discovered that, every year, after speaking to many packed stadiums and arenas around the country, my favorite and most fulfilling presentation were with those 400 eighth graders, so I made a decision to fill my schedule with high school and middle schools. My peers in the speaking profession were baffled. Why would I give up the big bucks and the prestige of speaking to professionals and corporations to speak to schools, many times at no charge? It was simply because of how fulfilling it was to speak to young minds. To realize that what you are saying may actually impact them personally. That you have the power to help shape how they feel and act.

I found my passion. I would tell my audiences that it was just as difficult to arrange to speak at a school for free as it was to land a commitment from a corporation or event planner to speak for a hefty speaking fee. But I found out a way to help schools reach out to me. I would ask my audiences to help open doors for me through the connections they had with the PTA, schools, and school districts. And it worked! I started having schools contact me to speak to their students. I found myself having a dream come true by being able to speak to students nationwide.

If you're reading this and can open a door, contact me. I found that a barrier that prevents too many people from not contacting me is the belief that I won't answer or get back to them, or the belief that I won't actually speak to their students because I'm too busy. Well, I'm telling you now, I will get back to you!

Speaking to young people made me realize how important social media is. One time a student remarked, “You’re nobody. You don’t have a following on Instagram.” I replied that I had spoken to over 5 million people live worldwide. But that didn’t mean anything to him. I was basically all talk unless I could prove it with a large following on social media, so I started asking my audiences to follow me at Bobmemory on Instagram to see if it helped my relationship with the student population.

Three years later I returned to that same junior high school. I asked the kids on the front row to check out Bobmemory on Instagram. With 10,000 followers, they said, “Wow, this is good!”

“What if I had three followers?” I asked.

“That would be bad,” they said. “Well, not bad, but it would mean you don’t know anybody.”

I said, “Really? You think I know 10,000 people?”

They said, “Yeah . . . uh . . . no, uh . . .”

My point is: How have we come to a place that followers determine our worth?

Ironically, the social media and cell phone problem is something that I speak on as a cause to anxiety problems. I teach that connection with each other is so much better for them than being connected electronically. If you're not convinced, try sending a hug in the form of a text. Does that have the same power of connection as a real hug? The cell phone and social media problem is affecting a countless number of organizations and institutes that rely on young people.

For instance, the Missionary Training Center in Provo, Utah, where thousands of young men and women, around eighteen to nineteen years old, prepare before they leave on missions, has a policy that individuals have to give up their smart phones. But they give some of the individuals dummy smart phones that don't do anything, in order to help them through the transition. It's kinda like giving a pacifier to a baby, just something to soothe and help calm them down.

I talked to an admiral in the Navy, who told me that, in boot camp, they know recruits are going to be a mess the first month because they pull the cell phones away from these kids. It's just something they're aware of now.

So, what's going on? Have you noticed the problem rising up around us? Do you see parents ignoring their children while they play on their phones? Do you see a bunch of kids out on a playground but not really playing anymore? They're all looking at their phones instead. Do you see teenagers sitting around a living room all playing on their phones? Walk anywhere, and you see this addiction that seems to be out of control.

Is it an addiction? There's an online test called "Are you addicted to your cell phone?" with questions like "Do you have to look at your cell phone before you go to bed?" "Is it the first thing you look at in the morning?" "Are you addicted to looking at Facebook and seeing what everybody else is doing?" "Are you afraid of missing out? That something is going on in the world, and you're going to miss it if you don't stay in touch?"

In a lecture, I heard a neuroscientist say, "The problem is we have a fifteenth-century brain overloaded with twenty-first-century technology. Every time you get a notification on your phone, every time you see a "like," what happens is you get a shot of dopamine, and just like a gambler, just like somebody who is drinking, it feels good."

That awareness just needs to arise. I spoke at Utah State University, and when I was through speaking, one of the administrators, one of the officials on campus, said, "That is the number-one hottest topic across the country right now: mental health." Instead of taking his word for it, I got online and I looked it up, and I went, *Oh my gosh, it is.* All across the country, it's happening. You want to find people that are depressed? Get on Facebook and look at the people who are posting continuously, day after day after day. There's something going on inside. Something's missing, and they're trying to find it through social connection instead of human connection.

Something you can do right now to help you start eliminating your cell phone addiction is to turn off all notifications. This is the first step, and it may not be so easy for some. One young man who was trying to get off his cell phone a couple of years ago told me that he kept feeling a phantom vibration in his pocket, and he learned that was his brain sending a message trying to get him to look at his phone. In fact, Simon Sinek talks about this problem of the brain craving the phone and sending signals to the body to look at it. He says it's the thing millennials are going to have to overcome. We are all losing the human connection because of this electronic connection.

My focus and message is no longer just about memory. It's about helping students, moms, dads, everyone achieve a better mind. And focusing on the human connection is key to achieving a better mind. The human connection is much stronger than an electronic connection.

***

So how exactly do you build a deeper human connection?

I learned along my journey that to deepen a relationship or build greater rapport, you must first understand that many individuals have walls up because they're wonder ing what you truly want. You have to set up an atmosphere where you don't want anything. You're just there to be with the other person. Genuine. Authentic. Connected.

If you find yourself in conversation with someone whose walls are up, consider revealing something from your past with no expectations. For example, if I just met a new speaker, I might comment, "I actually used to deal with massive panic attacks after my speaking events. Most professional speakers would never admit to experiencing something like that. They might want you to believe that they're perfect and they've got their lives together. Well, I'm not perfect and I don't always have everything together."

Now, when I share that story about myself to this new speaker I just met, or any individual, what happens? Their walls immediately drop because I revealed something authentic about myself. And now they feel more comfortable with me in conversation.

Always remember to be genuine, to be yourself. I have always loved learning something new and sharing it with others. I'm sure I drive some people insane by always showing up with a new story or excited about some new concept or idea that I came across that week. I started a "One Minute with Bob" series on Facebook, Instagram, and YouTube to start sharing with my audience some thoughts and lessons I've learned in life. When I learn something new, I like to share it with others.

Focusing on the human connection, making others feel more comfortable with you in conversation, remembering someone's name, and using the Power of Pause in conversation are all aspects that work toward something I call "the human side of people."

Why is remembering people's names so important to our success? The fact is, people can be unpleasant, irritating, negative, but have you ever noticed that it's pretty hard to do business without them? It is critically important in life to understand and appeal to "the human side of people." In fact, as a keynote speaker, I speak regularly about dealing effectively with people by understanding their "human side."

"The human side of people" is the irrational, funny, grumpy, loving, sad, happy, reactive, unpredictable side in all of us. It's the side of us that responds to our name when someone remembers and uses it. It's the side of people we do business with. It's the side of us that can tell when someone is actually listening to us and not just hearing us. The human side of people is in fact my most important topic. Helping you achieve great things through people by successfully dealing with their human side is my primary purpose for helping you develop a powerful memory. Memory will help you always remember the names of those you meet and all the things they share with you that are important to them. Understanding that people want to feel important is vital to understanding the human side of people. If you can master the human side of people, you will truly make a positive, enduring difference in the lives of your fellow human beings.

CHAPTER TWELVE

Enhance Your Human Connections. Enhance Your Life.

"I told my son I feel lost. He replied, 'Let me help you out, Dad. You're sitting right there.'"

—Bob Kittell

There are times I reflect back on my life and ask myself, *How did I get here?* How was I able to overcome so much and be so blessed to be in the current position I am in? I get to travel all over the nation teaching many different kinds of crowds about memory training and mindfulness. I truly love what I do.

However, there have been some situations in my life that I thought I would never get through. There was once a twenty-eight-day stretch where I was making preparations for my funeral.

The doctor told me that the small tumor he had removed was a metastatic adenocarcinoma, and that I had less than a year to live. What if you got the news that you had a year or less to live? How would you feel? What would you do?

The book *Prison to Praise* by Merlin Carothers states that it's easy to be grateful when things are going well, but not so much when things are falling apart. And I now found myself choosing how I was going to handle my last year of life. I picked up my video camera, walked outside, and started recording a message for my kids to see one day.

"Kids, I just found out I have a year to live, and I want you to know that I'm grateful for every day I have left with you."

Then I got practical. I called my dentist and canceled my appointment. I thought, *Well, that's one good thing: I don't have to go to the dentist any longer.*

A few days later, my fourteen-year-old daughter came to me very concerned and said, "Dad I have a question. Do you have life insurance?"

I was perplexed. "Yes. Why?"

"Is there any chance I can get some of that money for clothes?"

I burst out laughing.

Twenty-eight days after the initial diagnosis, the Huntsman Cancer Center called. The doctor, a specialist for this type of cancer, said, "I almost never get to tell people good news, but I think I have some for you."

He told me that my symptoms didn't make sense, so they decided to look at the whole tumor instead of just a slice. When they noticed a nerve coming out of the mass, they realized it was a benign neuroma—and I was okay.

That was a tough twenty-eight days. It was also a great twenty-eight days. When you are in a hard place, you just might be in the middle of your next inspirational chapter of life. I know I was. Something happened during that twenty-eight-day period that taught me one of my greatest life lessons. I learned from a wonderful little thirteen-year-old girl what a great and positive impact we can have on those who are going through a tough time.

My neighbor, Jocelyn, was thirteen years old—and going through chemotherapy for a brain tumor. When she heard about my situation, she took action. One day, she showed up at my door with a plate of cookies. Then she said the words that changed my life, "Mr. Kittell, you call me anytime day or night. I know what you're going through, and I think I can help."

Wow. I felt my perspective shift. This thirteen-year-old, dealing with her own struggles, knew how to make a difference. What was I doing with my life? More importantly, what was I doing to contribute to the lives of others? That is the real question, isn't it?

I began to ask that question of myself every morning. *Whose life can I change today?* Then I would spend the day trying to find that person. Sometimes that person may be a part of an audience of thousands in the New York Convention Center. Sometimes it's just one person I meet on a college campus or in an airport while waiting for a flight.

Students are always on my radar to help change their lives because they all share a common problem and goal. Their goal is to graduate. Their problem is the challenge to remember what they are taught and what they have read. Could I help? Of course I could! I could reach out. If Jocelyn could do it, so could I.

On a flight to a speaking engagement, I turned to a young lady sitting next to me and said, "You look like a student. Are you a student?"

"Yes."

"What's your challenge when it comes to memory?"

"Well, right now I gotta memorize a hundred flags of the world."

"I teach student how to memorize all kinds of information. Would you like me to show you how to quickly memorize all the flags of the world?"

"Sure!"

"Okay, let's try this. Show me a flag that you have to remember. That one? Turkey? Okay. Look at that flag and tell me what the first part is that catches your eye."

"Well, Turkey has a crescent and star . . . so I guess the star."

The country is Turkey, right? "Visualize a big, fat turkey eating the star. Gobble, gobble. Try it."

She got interested and excited. "What about a country like Cypress? How could I remember that flag?"

"Let's look at the flag. What catches your eye?"

"The middle of the flag," she said, "It looks like a swordfish."

"Okay, now when you say the word *Cypress*, what does that look like, sound like, or what does it remind you of?"

"How about a press? Like a printing press."

"Great. Now let's put the two together. How about a swordfish that has been flattened by a printing press?"

"Wow!"

"Okay, what's another one? The flag of Aruba? What's the first thing that catches your eye?"

"The two yellow lines."

"What does Aruba look like, sound like, or remind you of?"

"A ruby."

"Okay, can you picture thousands of rubies stuck on the two yellow lines?"

It worked. She was amazed that a complete stranger could help her with a project like this, without her even asking. I look for opportunities like this all the time, every day I want to change a life.

Another student told me she had to remember the names of seventy-five works of art and the artists associated with them. I taught her a memory trick specifically for this. I helped another student learn the twenty-seven amendments to the Constitution of the United States in less than twenty minutes.

Can you imagine how rewarding it is to see a student's eyes light up as they experience what feels like a brand-new part of their brain switching on? Can you imagine how gratifying it is to hear them say, "You just changed my life!"?

The cool thing is that, in just a minute or two, you facilitate a change in others that will always be with them; a new realization of their mental capacity; a new understanding of what they are capable of. And it doesn't just impact that one person or the thousands of individuals in your audience. If you change one person's life, they pass it on to impact the lives of others. As Scott Adams said, "There's no such thing as a small act of kindness. Each act creates a ripple with no logical end."

And that is why I now want to share with you one of my most advanced memory techniques, so I can impact your life, and then you can pass it on to impact the lives of others. Let the rippling effect begin!

Do you remember earlier how I convinced Coach Edwards to let me teach the football team memory skills? And how I remembered a page out of the phone book to convince him? Well, I used a system called the Phonetic System. This system is a very versatile and effective tool for remembering numbers.

Simply stated, the Phonetic System converts numbers into words. For example, if a friend were to walk up and say: "Hey, it's good to see you. Here's my phone number. Give me a call sometime at 915-7404." Wouldn't it be nice to just visualize a battle cruiser to remind you of the number 915-7404? Or remember an important extension number (854) by simply visualizing a flower? Or remember an appointment with the dentist at 3:27 by imagining a mink at the dentist? Or remember your bank account number by visualizing your bank being located in Constantinople, which stands for the number 720,121,295? You're probably wondering what the heck I'm talking about.

The Phonetic System is simply a number-to-letter code. Each of the numbers or digits from zero to nine is represented by a consonant sound. These consonant sounds can then be combined with vowels to form a word, which can be visualized. Once the code has been mastered, a whole new memory filing system can be explored. Let's start at the beginning.

PHONETIC RULES

RULE 1: In the Phonetic System, the consonant sounds are what is important, not the letters themselves.

RULE 2: Vowels (*a*, *e*, *i*, *o*, *u*, and the letters *w*, *h*, *y*) are only used to help build words; these letters will have no numerical value whatsoever.

RULE 3: Numbers 0–9 are represented by the following consonant sounds:

0) *s*, *z*, soft *c* (as in *cider*)
1) *t*, *d*
2) *n*
3) *m*
4) *r*
5) *l*
6) *sh*, *ch*, *j*, soft *g* (as in *germ*)
7) *k*, hard *c* (as in *cold*)
8) *v*, *f*
9) *p*, *b*

RULE 4: Silent letters are disregarded. For example: *knee* is a 2 (not 72), *bomb* is 93 (not 939), *phone* is 82 (not 92).

RULE 5: Double letters are used once. For example: *patter* is 914 (not 9114), *mummy* is 33 (not 333).

The number 1 is represented by the phonetic sound associated with the letters *t* or *d*. The word *tie* represents the number 1 since t represents the 1 and the vowels *i* and *e* have no value. The word *tot* is the number 11 because *t* represents a 1 for every *t* sound in the word.

Here are some examples of common words represented by numbers:

0) saw, zoo, sea, house, ace, ice
1) tie, dye, toy, wheat, hood
2) knee, Noah, honey, hyena, hen
3) ma, hymn, ham, mow, hem
4) rye, hare, oar, arrow, ore, wire, ray
5) law, ail, oil, owl, eel, halo, whale
6) shoe, joy, witch, jaw, jay, hedge
7) cow, cue, oak, hawk, wig, key, ivy
8) hoof, wave, hive, wife
9) bee, ape, pie, hoop, pea, boy, bay

Using the Phonetic System requires a little bit of brain power because you have to fill in the vowels. But once you use this system a few times, it will get easier and easier.

Let's try a quick exercise: You ran into a potential business associate, and he gives you his phone number—641-9410. How will you remember it until you can get to a place to write it down?

6 = *sh*

4 = *r*

1 = *t, d*

9 = *b*

4 = *r*

1 = *d*

0 = *s*

If you fill in the vowels, you have the phrase "short birds" for the number 641-9410. Isn't "short birds" easier to remember than a sequence of numbers? Once you have the consonant chart down, you will be able to remember any number, no matter how long it is! This is one of the more advanced memory techniques, but with practice, it can easily be mastered.

***

As I have shared my life story with you, you have probably seen the direct progression from one place in my life leading to the next, to the next, until I arrived at the place I am now. As I have said before, when opportunities arise, you must be prepared and take action. But that doesn't mean that every opportunity has to be building directly toward an end. Sometimes the best opportunities are just standalone pieces of your life. And that doesn't make them any less significant.

When I was having trouble getting a football scholarship at

BYU, I decided to try out for a school musical. I was in a beginning acting class, and students received extra credit for every production they auditioned for, regardless of the outcome. That sounded like a good deal. I could succeed just by trying to do something. Even if I failed, I would succeed by getting the extra credit, so I signed up for the auditions. I was not prepared. I had no clue as to how the process worked. I had inadvertently signed up for the biggest campus production of the year. When I showed up for the audition, I was surprised to see that there were dozens of trained actors and actresses trying out for this important musical production.

My name was called. I stepped to the center of the room facing the director, the choreographer, and everyone else who would determine who got in and who didn't.

The director said, "What have you prepared?"

"Prepared?"

"Yes. What are you going to sing?"

"Sing?"

"Yes."

I hesitated. "I didn't know we were supposed to . . . Was I supposed to have a song prepared?"

"Well, this *is* a musical."

"I have two weaknesses when it comes to musicals: I can't sing and I can't dance," I replied.

"You can't sing? So what are you doing here?"

"I'm just here because I was told I would get extra credit for my beginning acting class."

Everyone laughed. The director then asked, "Well, do you know any song well enough to sing it?"

"Not really. Nothing comes to mind."

"Why don't you sing a church hymn?"

"I don't know any church hymns."

Laughter kept coming from all around. I was beginning to look like a stand-up comic with no clue but a lot of nerve.

"Is there any song you do know?"

"Well . . ." I paused thoughtfully. "I know 'Doe a Deer,' you know, from *The Sound of Music*."

"Okay, let's go with that."

The music started and I started prancing around the stage like a deer, singing (a bit off key), "Doe, a deer, a female deer . . ."

The entire room was in stitches. Did I mention I can't sing? How about that I can't dance? No experience or talent with either, and I got the part. I didn't even know what part, but they cast me in this major campus production where I got to perform in front of thousands over a two-week run.

Everyone told me what a big deal it was that I was in this production, and what an honor that as a beginner I was picked. I'm still clueless as to why I was selected. I was just having fun.

This was a rare instance of no preparation leading to a great opportunity. My life took me in a different direction, but I still look back at this short time performing in this musical and am glad I was involved with it. Maybe it helped my confidence onstage. Maybe it helped me be okay speaking in front of large audiences. Maybe it helped me with nothing. But it was still a great life experience that I will always have. I want to encourage everyone to go out and experience life.

Everyone is at a different point in their life. But you don't have to be at a specific point to apply the practices and techniques you have learned in this book. You now know several memory techniques, so use them!

- Use the Linking System to remember any kind of list.
- Use the Image Method to remember someone's name.
- Use the Anatomy Method to remember items by placing them on your body.
- Use the Resemblance Peg System to associate items to numbers.
- Use the Loci System to remember items by placing them at certain spots.
- Use the Phonetic System to remember any number, no matter how large.

But memory training is only a part of this book. To master your mind, you have to recognize your past troubles. You cannot move forward in your life if you are holding onto grudges. Let the grudges go so you can prosper. If you have shameful memories in your past, face them and then set them free. Doing so will clear your mind and allow you to view the world in a new way. Stop playing "movies" in your mind over and over again. It's taking up too much of your time and causing unnecessary anxiety.

You have also learned how to connect with people. Always remember someone's name. You have no excuse now that you have a memory technique for this! Use the Power of

Pause in conversation, and just watch your connection build with the person you are talking to. It's easy to make someone more comfortable with you in conversation; just be genuine with them by sharing something personal about yourself. Their walls will instantly drop, allowing the two of you to make a connection.

Memory techniques are extremely useful, and they definitely help boost your mind power. But eliminating negative matter from your mind is also key, and connecting with people is equally, if not more, important.

Do you truly wish to enhance your life and the lives of others? Then focus on being mindful of them. Improve your memory with the use of the memory skills described in this book so that you can actually connect better. Enhance that connection by actually paying attention to, and remembering, their name and what is important to them.

It seems a simple thing, but just being more mindful of—and actually remembering—what is important to others is critically important in today's world. It is the mark of a successful leader on campus, in business, and in life. Being remembered and appreciated (valued) is one of the greatest human needs—more important even than being loved. Therefore, remembering

others names, and what is important to them, and thereby making them feel important, is one of the simplest, yet greatest skills in creating powerful and long lasting social, political, and business connections.

Try it – and enjoy the powerful difference it makes in their lives and in yours.

***

For more information on Bob, visit **www.bobkittell.com**